AF505443

Collaborative Development in Northeast Asia

Collaborative Development in Northeast Asia

Michio Morishima
STICERD
London School of Economics and Political Science

Translated by

Janet Hunter
Saji Senior Lecturer
London School of Economics and Political Science

 First published in Great Britain 2000 by
MACMILLAN PRESS LTD
Houndmills, Basingstoke, Hampshire RG21 6XS and London
Companies and representatives throughout the world

A catalogue record for this book is available from the British Library.

ISBN 0–333–74893–X

 First published in the United States of America 2000 by
ST. MARTIN'S PRESS, LLC,
Scholarly and Reference Division,
175 Fifth Avenue, New York, N.Y. 10010

ISBN 0–333–74893–X

Library of Congress Cataloging-in-Publication Data
Morishima, Michio, 1923–
    Collaborative development in Northeast Asia / Michio Morishima ; translated
    by Janet Hunter.
        p. cm.
    Includes bibliographical references and index.
    ISBN 0–333–74893–X
    1. East Asia—Economic conditions. 2. Economic forecasting—East Asia. I.
    Title.

    HC460.5 .M658 2000
    338.95—dc21
                                                                    00–062616

This book is printed on paper suitable for recycling and made from fully managed and sustained forest sources.

10   9   8   7   6   5   4   3   2   1
09 08 07 06 05 04 03 02 01 00

Printed and bound in Great Britain by
Antony Rowe Ltd, Chippenham, Wiltshire

Contents

Preface   vii

Introduction: Revisiting China After 54 Years   1

Lecture 1 – The Hostile Relationship in Northeast Asia   21

Lecture 2 – Vicissitudes of Nations: A Materialist View   61

Lecture 3 – The Dawn of Asia   97

Lecture 4 – Northeast Asia's Future   129

Notes   164

Index   170

Preface

It is painful for Japanese to make a proposal, to China, Korea and other Asian peoples, for collaboration between Asian countries. This stems from the fact that in 1943 the Tojo government of Japan summoned the leaders of Asian countries to Tokyo to make them support Japan's idea of the Greater East Asian Co-Prosperity Sphere. This co-prosperity did not mean, however, prosperity of Asian countries on an equal basis; rather these countries were more or less forced to come under the sway of Japan. During the Second World War, in fact, Singapore was decleared a city in the territory of Japan, and referred to as *Shonan City*.

Much earlier than this imperialist movement, there had been many examples of sincere collaboration between Japanese and Chinese. Such great Chinese figures as Sun Yat-sen, Chiang Kai-shek, Zhou En-lai, Lu Xin, Guo Ruo-mo and many others had either stayed in Japan for a considerable time or studied there, and many of them enjoyed warm and respectful friendships with the Japanese. Unfortunately, this sincere tradition of friendly relations was entirely destroyed as soon as the Japanese army killed the generalissimo of the Manchuria area of China in 1928.

Despite this difficulty, in Autumn 1997 I delivered to students of Nankai University a series of lectures proposing the establishment of a Northeast Asian Economic Community. The students addressed understood the necessity of such a community in this period of globalization of transportation and communication. They were very positive and serious to an extent that could not be matched by Japanese students. One of them even decided to come to London, and is now at LSE, where I work.

This book brings together four of the Nankai Lectures. They are all corrected, modified and even expanded greatly, because the audience is not now confined to Chinese students but opened to the general readers of this book. In spite of the unfortunate history of the past, the countries of Northeast Asia have a more or less similar ethos. They have been competitive with each other for a very long period, which in my view means that they can also be good collaborators.

Finally I am indebted to Janet Hunter, LSE, for the translation of this work and would like to express my gratitude to her.

MICHIO MORISHIMA

Introduction: Revisiting China After 54 Years

I

In September, 1997, I visited China at the invitation of Nankai University in Tianjin. I had visited China on several occasions while I was at middle and high school, and at university, but my last visit had been in April 1943. These visits had been because my father was working on the staff of Chinese Airlines in Beijing, and my mother and elder sister had accompanied him to live in Beijing. Chinese Airlines was a joint Sino-Japanese concern, but was in effect a national policy company under the control of the Japanese government. After December 1941, Japan had not only invaded China, but was, of course, also at war with Britain and the United States. My mother insisted on their returning to Japan, and my father agreed to this. He in fact returned to Japan a little in advance of the others, as my mother was ill, and stayed in Beijing with my sister. I was in my first year at university at the time. During the spring vacation I went to Beijing, and returned to Japan, bringing with me my sister, and my mother, who had now recovered. For 54 years from that time I made no visit to China. A feeling of guilt that our residence in Beijing was closely associated with Japan's aggression in China was a factor in keeping me from revisiting the country.

Although Tianjin was on the way to Beijing, I had never once visited the city on the seven or eight occasions that I had been to Beijing in the past. For that reason I knew very little about Nankai University except that it was one of China's leading universities after Beijing, Qinghua, and Fudan Universities, and that it was the university attended by

1

Zhou Enlai. I did remember, however, that the 1940 *Review of Economic Studies* had contained a comment on Hicks' *Value and Capital* (1939) by C. M. Li, who was at the time professor at Nankai University, which had been evacuated to Zhongqing. The editor of the *Review* published Li's comment as he thought in the following way:

> Professor Li's point is very similar to that raised by Professor Lange (cf. *Review of Economic Studies*, October 1940). But it is clear that Professor Lange's note and Professor Hicks' reply had not penetrated to Zhongqing when Professor Li wrote his note. It is felt that in view of all the circumstances the note will be of considerable interest to readers of the *Review*.

This is sufficient ground for supposing that in those days the international popularity of economics in China may well have been considerably higher than in Japan. (After the war Li worked at the United Nations, and was then employed at the University of California, before returning to Nankai University in his later years. He lived to an old age, but I was never managed to get to meet him.) It is true that Nankai University was inferior to Beijing University in terms of buildings and other facilities, but reminded me of Hokkaido University, one of the seven former imperial universities that still exist in Japan.

Before my wife and I went to Tianjin, we stayed for two nights in Beijing. After landing at Beijing Airport I found myself continually comparing the city of Beijing with what it had been 54 years earlier. Beijing Station had at that time been right next to the city's main gate, and on its east side there was a special rectangular-shaped area, with its longer sides east–west, and its shorter sides north–south. This was the area in which all the foreign embassies were located. The area was surrounded by a broad, hook-shaped belt of grass. This grass was carefully mown like a football pitch, and looked beautiful. However, the main purpose of its existence was to enable the troops to machine gun the Chinese masses as they ran across the open grass, should violence break out and the embassies come under attack. In fact all of the embassies had their own troops stationed there.

In strong contrast with this were the slums on the southern side of the main gate. The city of Beijing was divided into two zones, known as the inner city (north of the main gate) and the outer city (south of the gate), each surrounded by its own walls. The inner city was the location of government offices and the expensive commercial districts, while the outer city was home to the poor lower classes with their small shops and stalls, and shabby red-light districts. This side-by-side existence of a beautiful Beijing and a run-down Beijing made me palpably aware of the pressures of imperialism. Since Beijing was at that time under Japanese occupation, imperialism effectively meant Japanese imperialism, and until Japan declared war on Britain and the United States towards the end of 1941 one could still feel a pervasive Western influence in the city. But, of course, for the Chinese people themselves, especially those in the Communist Party, this kind of a Beijing was only a symbol of their humiliation.

Under Mao Zedong major changes were made in Beijing. The two sets of city walls were demolished, and Beijing Station moved to a new location on the southeast side of the former embassy area. The embassy area itself, of course, was also totally demolished, and the green belt surrounding it ceased to exist. In all likelihood sensible Chinese at that time welcomed such measures, and were left feeling satisfied with what had been done. The slums, moreover, were swept away, and the outer city area was transformed into a splendid commercial zone and place for small and medium-sized enterprises. These were extremely praiseworthy achievements.

The result of all this was that apart from buildings such as the old imperial palace, the only thing that recalled to mind the Beijing of 54 years earlier was the building of the Beijing Hotel, which had been on the eastern side beyond the green belt that had enclosed the embassy area. It had never been enormous but it was a luxury level hotel. On the first floor had been a small bookshop that sold Western books, and I had bought there Joan Robinson's *Essays in the Theory of Employment* and Gustav Cassel's *Fundamental Thoughts in Economics*. The hotel, however, had been greatly expanded, and it retained very little of its former external appearance or its internal set-up. The lobby now is darker than I recall its having been before, but the tea shop was lovely and comfortable.

My father's house was in a northeastern part of Beijing's inner city known at the time as Inner Third Quarter. It would take me about an hour to walk back to the house from Beijing Station. The moving of the station to the east meant that the new station was much nearer. I took a bus from the hotel where I was staying to the new railway station, and began to walk from there, under the impression that I would be able to reach our old house without any difficulty. It turns out, however, that I was not as fit as I had been 54 years ago. I was flagging long before I reached the edge of the Eleventh Hutong, where the house had been. 'Let's take a break somewhere. I'm hungry too', I said to my wife, and we went into a dumpling shop on the corner where Eleventh Hutong met Dongsi Bdj.

The shop was a specialist dumpling shop. It was full of young people enjoying their midday meal and talking loudly. We also liked dumplings. My wife tried to order using the Japanese term *gyoza*, but could not make herself understood. We tried changing the pronunciation, and gesticulated to try and get the meaning of *gyoza* through, but the waitress's expression remained one of not understanding. I remembered that my mother had used the word *chaozu*; so I tried that and she immediately understood. When she asked how many we wanted my wife spread out her hands and said 'ten'. Once again the waitress did not understood. Thinking that she did not understand that 'ten' meant 10, my wife counted out the number on her fingers, and finally said 'ten' again, but it did not seem to do any good.

We were at a total loss, and I looked at the menu to see whether there might be anything else, but since it was a specialist dumpling shop, the only variety was in the fillings of the dumplings, and there was nothing else where the issue of 'ten' could be avoided. I did make, however, one important discovery. The menu gave the unit price of each item, and in each case it was written in the form of so many dollars (*yuan*) and cents (*que*) per unit of weight. The weight was measured in *kin* (1.33 lb), the Chinese pound, but we did not know how many *kin*'s worth of dumplings two people would eat. My wife said that she had no idea, and neither of us wanted to be the one to order. So I asked my wife to say to the waitress that we would have however many we were given. 'If that's the case, why don't you say it yourself?', she said. So on the table I inscribed with my finger the Chinese character for 'half' on the table, and using the Japanese pronunciation *pan kin*. She certainly understood. We did have more than we could eat, but *pan kin* was a quantity not too far off the mark. (Later on we ate dumplings in a hotel in Shanghai, but on that occasion the words *pan kin* were not understood at all. The unit was six or twelve dumplings, i.e. half a dozen, or a dozen. Whether this was a difference between the internationalism of Shanghai and the traditionalism of Beijing, or whether it was simply a regional distinction between North and Central China, I have no way of knowing.)

II

After that we began to look for my parents' old house. Round about where I thought the house had been there were buildings including an oblong local authority office, or a primary school, and the appearance of the street had changed. I thought that my parents' house had probably been demolished to make way for these buildings. Since the residences owned by a Japanese airline would have been returned to the Chinese government, there was every likelihood that the government itself, or the city of Beijing, would have removed such confiscated property, replacing it with public buildings. However, the thought that if it no longer existed the trouble that we had taken to walk all the way from the new Beijing Station had been totally wasted drove me to continue searching for an alternative, separate house, as a second possibility. I then peeped through the gates of several houses, as my father's house had had a large gate.

My wife said: 'It's no good. What are you going to do if someone asks you why you are creeping around like a thief?'. Almost at the same time a middle-aged woman from inside the gate started to cross-examine me. I told her in English that because I had used to live here, I had wanted to come back and look around. (Everything said by me below was spoken in English.) The woman did not understand English, so while I was speaking English I used Chinese characters to explain the meaning of what I was saying. She responded in the same way, by writing character:

> 'Please explain what sort of a house yours was.'
> 'It was a big house, with another family living in the front part. There was a large ballroom in the middle, which we used as a storeroom. Beyond was my father's house, which had a very wide corridor around it, . . . and a large garden as well.'
> 'About how wide was the corridor?'
> 'Around 3 metres.'
> 'That much?'

I thought that her 3 metres was rather short, but said that that was roughly right. The woman's attitude changed quickly.

> 'Please come and have a look. I will show you to the entrance of your house.'

With these words, she went ahead of us.

This house had a large gate, and was divided into two sections to right and left of the driveway looking in from the gate. On the right hand side was the woman's house, and behind it 'my father's house'. On the left-hand side a jumble of small houses had been built, with winding narrow paths between one house and the next. As I was wondering what would happen if there were ever a fire, the woman turned to the right, and then to the left. There had also been a lot of small houses opposite my father's house. They had been the housing for younger staff of the company, and had been rebuilt in the style of Japanese longhouses (*nagaya*). I don't remember very well, since I hardly ever went in them, but I certainly did not think that it had been such a maze as this. However, the maze finally brought us to the side gate of a house which I could imagine had been my father's house. The recollection came to me that the actual side door of the house had very much resembled this one.

I expressed my thanks to her, and followed the maze back to reach her house. Her husband came out. He was a dentist and said that he had his surgery here. He asked when we had been living here, since they themselves had been here for 30 years, so I told him that it had been 54 to 58 years previously. He gave a kind of shriek, and wrote on the paper the words 'venerable age'. I realized how time had passed quickly.

Leaving the house, I said to my wife: 'So, I am of a venerable age now. I didn't know there was such an expression'. She pressed me for an answer to her question as to whether it really was that house. Being shocked at realizing my age (I was 74 years old at that time), I could only reply to my wife by saying that my sister might well remember, so we would try and ask her when we got back to Japan before the final voyage to London. I, however, had become of a venerable age, even though it only seemed to me like a few years had passed. Certainly it was 54 years since my last visit to China, when I had returned for the final time to Beijing to bring my mother back to Japan after her illness, so this was a period equivalent to two-thirds of my long life up to the present. As far as I was concerned it was less the inability to find the house than the shock of being told that I was of a venerable age that had upset me. I brought back the conversation to my wife's question, and replied that I did not think that it was that house, but it would be the one, if I should choose one from among those remaining along the Eleventh Hutong.

Apart from the removal of the city walls and the demolition of the embassy area, the Inner City area of Beijing has not changed a great deal. Naturally new and splendid buildings have been constructed everywhere. All these buildings are shiny-clean, and in no way inferior by comparison with those in the capitals of richer countries. I am greatly saddened, however, by the removal of the city walls. If it had been up to me, I would probably have left the Inner City area as it was, including both the walls and the embassy area. Since there are large areas of land outside the city, it would have been possible to build a totally new capital. If that had been done it would have been possible to make a clear comparison between the old and new capitals, enabling the Communist government to display its achievements. The embassy quarter could, moreover, have become an important teaching resource for the people of the future. As for the slums of the Outer City, I, too, would have removed them. It would be enough to display photographs of them in a museum as a way of teaching people about their history.

III

There are two characteristics that are associated with China. The first is the view of the country that sees it in its entirety as a fortified nation state, surrounded by a great wall. The second is the perspective of Chinese philosophy, that views China as the centre of the world, and is fully aware of its own superiority. Both of these views are widely held, but my own view is that it is the former view, rather than the latter, that accords with China's history. The capitals of China were initially located in the region of the Yellow River. Sian was the starting point of the Silk Road, and it was here that the eleven dynasties had their capital. The nine dynasties, starting with the Zhou, established their capital in Loyang, to the east of Sian, while further to the east, in Gaifeng, was the capital of the seven dynasties. China's capital thus gradually moved from the interior towards the east, and nearer to the coastal area.

It was around 1153, under the Jin, that the capital was moved to Beijing. After the Jin, the Yuan, Ming and Qing all had their capitals there. During that period of 758 years up to the fall of the Qing in 1911, of the four dynasties that ruled China, neither the Qin, the Yuan nor the Qing were of the Chinese Han people. All of them were peoples from north of the Great Wall. The Ming, who were Han people, were in power for 304 years, so Beijing was for the remaining 454 years under the rule of those thought of as 'barbarians'. This would not seem to have been conducive to the concept of a so-called Chinese empire. However, despite this the Chinese themselves did during that period continue to regard China as a Chinese empire, and the country continued to be perceived as such by other countries as well.

In actual fact it was a country ruled by foreigners. And finally, just for a few years, it was even invaded by a savage tribe from the east, the barbarian country of Japan. If we think about it in this way, then we can say that the first Qin emperor was quite right to construct the Great Wall to defend the Han people from barbarian tribes. It was certainly not a needless defence policy. Despite its existence, however, China was repeatedly subjected to the ravages of barbarian tribes. It was to try and pre-empt this reality that the Great Wall was built. China made desperate efforts to try and protect the territory of the Han people, and channelled the nation's energies into this project. The emphasis on China as the country of the Great Wall certainly sheds a considerable light on that particular aspect of Chinese history. However, in addition to being overrun by barbarians, China also had to confront the reality of its situation, which meant, at least superficially, having to respect these barbarians, and having to deal appropriately with them. Thus the capital of China, from the earliest times of Sian, became a cosmopolitan city, a city in which both foreign cultures and Han culture could prosper side by side.

This is true even by comparison with the recent experience of the Japanese. Until the period of the Second World War, when Japan had never had to surrender to any other country, Japanese cities were overflowing with classical atmosphere, but since Japan's defeat Tokyo and the other major cities have become totally cosmopolitan. This kind of situation has existed in China since ancient times, but the Chinese have regarded it as part of being Chinese. China's embodiment of openness, and not exclusionism, constituted the nucleus of thought in China, what was referred to as Chinese Nationalism. This pragmatic aspect of Chinese thought was diametrically opposed to the common theory that the national thought calls for Chinese world dominance. For that reason it is a mistake to think of China to conceptualize China as a nation of Chinese thought. Though my stay in China this time was very short, I did find during my visit a very broad-minded sense of internationalism among members of China's intelligentsia.

There are many Westerners and Japanese who think of China as a communist country, whose people are dogmatic and uncompromising, and whose ideology is incapable of flexibility, but Chinese people are, in actual fact, both optimists and realists. If they were not, they would not have been able to survive for more than two thousand years in a country subject to repeated revolutions and the harsh vicissitudes of dynasties. This is in strong contrast to the case of the Japanese, with their belief in what was claimed to be 'the unbroken line of the imperial family coeval with heaven and earth'. From a historical perspective, it is the Japanese who are the ideologists, and the Chinese who are the realists.

During the period from the end of the sixth century to the beginning of the eighth century, when the Japanese state was being established, China was in the midst of a period of upheaval. The Sui unified China, but 29 years later saw the rise of the Tang and the overthrow of the Sui. In Japan at the time there co-existed two states, the country of Wa (the Kyushu dynasty), and the country of Nihon (Japan) (the Yamato dynasty). When Paekche was attacked by the Tang, the country of Wa, which had strong bonds of friendship with Paekche, sent troops to Korea to support Paekche, but suffered a major defeat at the hands of the Tang navy in a battle at the Paekson River.

The country of Nihon, too, advanced troops as far as Kyushu, but its attitude toward the conflict was rather negative. According to Professor Takehiko Furuta, 'it is written in the local chronicles of Bitchu region that, taking advantage of the death of the Saimei Emperor, who had advanced as far as Asakura in Chikushi, Prince Naka no Oe and his followers withdrew their forces, on the grounds of having to observe the mourning ceremonies'. The same thing can be read in the *Nihon Shoki*. Through this negative policy, Nihon resisted being drawn into the war. Paekche was destroyed and Wa too suffered severely, with the result that Nihon, which had retained a neutral stance, remained intact, and before long was able to swallow up the declining country of Wa (Yamatai-koku). (There are no established theories relating to the history of that time, but it is this theory of Furuta's that I think is the most persuasive of the several that have been put forward.) The country of Nihon, having experienced such circumstances as these during its foundation, was inevitably vigilant, defensive and conservative. The people of Nihon were horrified at the thought of revolution. This attitude was in very strong contrast to that of the

Chinese, with their notion that a dynasty that had lost the mandate of heaven was bound to be replaced by another one. The Japanese of that time believed that Nihon would for ever be ruled over by an imperial family, and fabricated a history (myth) that said that emperors had also ruled Nihon in the past from the beginning of time – despite the fact that Nihon was a late starting country, established after the Kingdom of Wa.

Therefore, while the Japanese people shared Confucianism with the Chinese, they were nationalistic (focused upon their ruler), as opposed to the humanitarianism (focused upon the people) of the Chinese. This difference is what has generated such a contrast in the fates of the two countries in the modern period. In the country created by the Japanese, with their fierce exclusionism and pride, there was no chance of building a capital such as that of China, which was like a cultural salon for the peoples of East Asia. Not until after the Second World War did Tokyo begin to become this kind of city. Imbued with their warlike spirit, the Japanese sought to disregard the people of other lands.

IV

In fact, in those distant times, there were in Japan a number of dynasties. The most powerful of these was the Wa, but, as we have seen above, the Wa were brought down and destroyed, to be absorbed by the kingdom of Nihon. Nihon subjugated other dynasties apart from Wa, to unify most of the country of Japan.

Relations between China, Korea and Wa at that time were extremely close. For one thing, geographically these countries are surprisingly close to each other in terms of distance. Between Korea and China lies the Yellow Sea. The Shandong peninsula sticks out from the continent, and opposite it, on the Korean peninsula, there protrudes towards it the region of Nakrang. The distance between the two is therefore not that great, not dissimilar to the distance between Greece and the southern tip of the Italian peninsula. To the north of this lies an enclosed sea, which can be thought of like a rather wider Adriatic. This sea, moreover, has been celebrated in martial songs as 'the mirror-like Yellow Sea', and is invariably calm. Just as Greek civilization crossed the sea to Rome, there is no doubt that the civilization of the Sui and the Tang crossed the sea to reach Nakrang.

The sea between Kyushu and southern Korea is much rougher, but since Tsushima, Iki and other islands lie between them, the passage is not too hard a one. The distance between Tsushima and Pusan is about the same as that between Hiroshima and Matsuyama, and between Hakata and Pusan roughly half the distance between Osaka and Beppu. Moreover, conclusions drawn from research on both the Korean and Japanese sides suggest that the people of Wa were a kind of seafaring tribe with bases in both Korea and Kyushu.

If this was, in fact, the case, it is likely that the Wa came under Sui and Tang influence at an early stage. If we compare Wa and Nihon (the Yamato dynasty) at the time, the latter was clearly more backward than the country of Wa. Wa suffered reverses, and was absorbed into Nihon. In the light of these circumstances, we can say that it was natural for the leaders of Nihon to turn their minds towards creating a national philosophy, so that they could implant in people's minds the kind of ideology that would prevent what had happened to Wa from ever happening to Nihon.

This led to the editing of the *Nihon Shoki* and *Kojiki* at the start of the eighth century. While they take the form of historical works, they are in fact the writings of a national philosophy that claims the existence of an imperial family coeval with heaven and earth ruling in an unbroken line. We also find that among the poems from that period in the *Man'yoshu,* there are a number which are concerned with the country, or praise the emperor – nationalistic poems – which is amazing for so early a period as the seventh and eighth centuries, but even so, this can be understood if we take into account their background of a period of crisis.

Japan's national awareness, which started with its sense of inferiority in relation to China, later on in Japanese history, at the time of the Yuan (Mongol) attack on Japan, became a spiritual imperative to defend the ancestral land. Over the next 700 years, however, it was not China and Korea that attacked Japan, but Japan who, without warning and without reason, launched an attack on them. These were Hideyoshi's two attacks on Korea, the Sino-Japanese War and annexation of Korea in the Meiji period, and the Manchurian Incident and war with China during the Showa period. Behind these there were the contrasting views of nation of China and Japan.

Even in the peaceful present, there are some Japanese who hold very inflexible views towards China, on the grounds that it is a communist country. I myself take the view that the Chinese people's perception of their nation has over the course of history proved flexible and evolving, while that of the Japanese has at the same time been arrogant and aggressive. It has, in short, been imperialistic, in the premodern sense of the word. We are fortunate that contemporary Japanese are extremely peaceful. However, should the depression continue, and Japan's international position deteriorate to that of a second or third rank nation, or worse, the country could find itself in the dangerous situation of 'chauvinistic patriots' appearing to stir up the people's inferiority complex to explosive levels, and the country may well once again embark on a course of violence as the wolf of Asia.

Looked at from the other way around, my view of Asia becomes the basis for looking at things along the following lines. Even in the seventh century, when means of transport were still undeveloped, there were close relations between China, Korea and Japan. Their contacts were not limited to the level of fighting each other, but they shared the same script, and to a considerable extent also had ideas in common. Moreover, the Japanese Abe no Nakamaro became a senior official of the Chinese government and was a major participant in activities there. The scale of such interaction may have been small, but there did exist a kind of Asian collectivity or community (or rather, there is evidence that such a thing was far from impossible). At Nankai University I put forward my argument that an option for Japan would be the proposal a Northeast Asian community as a vehicle for Asian economic activity.

The impasse in which Asian growth finds itself is due to the deadlock in the Japanese economy; if a solution can be found for Japan's economic trouble, the problem of unsecured assets and financial crisis can be solved. The concept of an Asian community can lead to major organizational changes for the various countries of Asia. Introducing this kind of innovation would serve to create effective demand in China, Taiwan and Korea as well as Japan.

V

While I was in China the national congress of the Chinese Communist Party was being held in Beijing. The congress concluded with the election of the seven members of supreme council of the party. The following day the papers contained both photographs and brief summaries of the careers of these men. From the English language paper, *China Daily*, I learnt first of all that the leader Jiang Zemin had been born into a family of the intellectual classes in 1926, had graduated from Shanghai Jiaotong University, and was a specialist in electrical engineering. I was surprised in two respects by this account of his career. There are two ways of class categorizations. First, people are categorized as landlord class, capitalist class, working class, bureaucracy and so on, using the class categories of a capitalist (or socialist) society. Secondly, in the Chinese style of class categorization the influence of Confucianism led to people being assigned a higher or lower status according to whether or not they had been in receipt of education. Jiang Zemin's class of origin was clearly identified from a Confucian perspective, and not from a communist perspective. For a Confucian to have been born into the intellectual class is something to be proud of, while surely for a member of the communist party it is something as far as possible to be concealed.

This was not just the case with Jiang. Talking to professors and students at Nankai University, I learnt that it was very rare for people to hide their class origins or occupation prior to the revolution. Quite a number of these individuals had been exposed to considerable hardship at the time of the Cultural Revolution as a result of their former class origins, and in fact, they included some whose parents had been persecuted, or even committed suicide. When I asked their assessment of Mao Zedong, they would always all agree that he was a great figure, but that even he had made major mistakes. My feeling is that they have not forgotten the sufferings at the time of the Cultural Revolution, but that they are prepared to forgive in the light of his outstanding achievements.

Next there is the issue of Jiang Zemin's university, the Shanghai Jiaotong University. 'Jiaotong' normally means in Japanese 'traffic' or 'transportation', or, more broadly, the mutual understanding and communication between one individual and another. However, while it is rare to use the word in this broader meaning in Japanese, in Chinese it is frequently used in this sense. Shanghai Jiaotong University is best translated into Japanese as Shanghai Information University. This makes Jiang's being a graduate of the electrical engineering and electronics departments more understandable. It is well known in China, moreover, that there are several other Jiaotong universities (many of which are offshoots of the Shanghai Jiaotong

University that have since become independent). Whatever the case, one is tempted to ask in which major countries of the world it is possible for the graduate of a science university to achieve the top position in politics. Jiang's university background shows that China is no ordinary communist state. Classifications of modern and ultra-modern are probably more appropriate to China than classifications such as capitalism and socialism.

On the other hand, Prime Minister Li Peng would seem to be an appropriate prime minister for a communist country. Born in 1928 into a family that had fallen victim to the revolution, he received his higher education in the Soviet Union. Li too, however, received a scientific education, specializing in electrical engineering. The deputy prime minister, Zhu Rongji was also born in 1928. This means that he would have graduated from university immediately after the establishment of the People's Republic of China, so he probably entered university before the Republic. He is a graduate of Qinhua University.

In Beijing there exist Beijing University, which specializes in the humanities, and Qinhua University, which specializes in the sciences. Both are illustrious universities. Zhu studied electrical engineering, specializing in telecomunications. He has been mayor of Shanghai, and is well known for drafting macroeconomic policies. He is widely regarded as Jiang Zemin's likely successor. The top three figures in the Chinese government, therefore, have thus all specialized in science, making it ultramodern by comparison with the governments of the G8 countries.

Of the remaining four members of the leadership, three were born in 1930, the other one in 1942. Three have been to university, two of them again graduating from science-related faculties (hydroelectric engineering and mechanical engineering). One is an alumnus of Qinhua University, the other of Liaodong Engineering School. Liaodong Engineering School can be seen as the successor of Liaodong Engineering University founded by the Japanese. The Japanese intention was to elevate this university at some point in the future to the status of Imperial University, and it is likely that even in China these institutions are regarded as being of considerable excellence. Only Li Ruihuan has graduated from a university associated with the humanities (Shanghai's Fudan University), where he specialized in international trade. Since the best humanities and social science graduates seem to be concentrated at Beijing, Fudan and Nankai universities, Fudan University, too, is extremely illustrious. The final individual of the group was born into a family of tenant farmers, and initially worked as a carpenter, although he afterwards studied part time at the School of Architectural Engineering in Beijing.

Thus six out of the seven Chinese leaders have received a scientific education, and all the six who have been to university have been to top institutions. Only two seem to have had the careers one might expect for a communist country. It is hardly conceivable that a group of this kind should engage in dogmatic, extreme left-wing politics. Given that their specialist scientific subjects were all aspects of engineering, they may be expected to be pragmatists. One might imagine that they would be likely to be rather progressive in temperament, and full of the entrepreneurial spirit. If this characterisation of China's leadership is correct, then the widespread view of China as being dominated by the Chinese Communist Party, that sees the party as an inflexible, dogmatic body, and the people as all brainwashed into accepting the party's beliefs (whether Marxism-Leninism, or Maoism), is utterly wide of the mark.

VI

I lectured at Nankai University along the lines of my book, *Options for Japan*, which was published in Japanese at the end of 1995 (Iwanami Contemporary Library). Since I believed at the time that under the current circumstances Japan would decline unless something was done, what I was suggesting was how Japan could be rescued. There seem to have been some people, however, who saw my proposal as resembling the establishment of the Great East Asia Co-Prosperity Sphere advocated by aggressive Japanese governments earlier this century, so I had to be careful about putting forward the same proposals in China. Moreover, since my proposal was for the establishment of a northeast Asian community, I also had to explain why this should be separate from southeast Asia. These points, however, did not cause any major problem. The real problem was one of 'one community, two systems', whether it was possible for Japan, Korea and Taiwan to form a community with China and North Korea, whose systems were totally different. At Nankai University I avoided addressing this question head-on, and instead talked about 'socialism with Chinese characteristics' (the Chinese style of socialism), which was a slogan of the Chinese government at that time.

What I argued was that the Chinese style of socialism closely resembles what I have called 'capitalism from above' elsewhere. At some point 'capitalism from above' has to encounter the question of selling off state enterprises to the private sector, as happened in Meiji Japan. If this process is unsuccessful, it is not possible for the state to achieve a higher economic level. This is the stage that China has now reached, and if the state enterprises can be successfully transformed into self-supporting, private sector enterprises, then the industrial belt along China's eastern coast is likely to develop substantially. At this stage the coastal zones must have very close connections with the resource-rich areas of the hinterland, and the country must be provided with ships and harbours to connect the coastal zones with the rest of the world. If China is to achieve this, the cooperation of Korea and Japan is absolutely indispensable.

I also stated the following:

> There is no doubt that during the war Japan perpetrated outrageous atrocities. We all know that individuals can suffer from insanity, but peoples, too, can go mad, and regrettably this was the situation in Japan through the 1930s and the first half of the 1940s. I think that Chinese people are likely to comprehend such a situation. (In fact, many of them seem to have listened to my 'theory of national insanity' while recollecting the latter stages of the Cultural Revolution.) The resolution of whether or not the five countries of northeast Asia (including Taiwan) can surmount the situation of one community – two systems to cooperate with each other – a decision which will determine the fates of our children and grandchildren – depends on our courage and resolve.

In mentioning the atrocities perpetrated by the Japanese army during the war, I had thought of using the word 'apology', but because I wanted to know their real feelings, I did not initially engage in apologies or the expression of regrets, as I wished to distance the issue as far as possible from any moral judgment. My ideas and genuine feelings got through to them, and I think that they accepted them. I drew this conclusion from the fact that, although I had predicted that the number of students attending the following day might fall, it did not go down. If anything it increased, and on the last two days the former president of Nankai University also attended.

After Nankai I visited Beijing University, as I had intended to do. I had not planned to give any lectures there, but when I arrived, I was unexpectedly asked by the head of the faculty to give a lecture. I was not quite sure what to do. Professor Lou Xianghe, who had accompanied me from Nankai, said that I could talk about the same things that I had lectured on at Nankai. Since I tend to forget what I have lectured about, and since I had not brought with me any of my notes, I racked my brains to try and remember what I had talked about at Nankai. Professor Lou reminded me that it had been about an Asian community, as if to rebuke me for my lack of responsibility. On this occasion students poured into the large lecture room, which was already almost full when I arrived. The room was located in a splendid new building donated by a Taiwanese businessman, and I was the first to use it. There must have been at least 150 students there.

I had thought that the welcome I received in China was the result of my book on *Marx's Economics* (1973), but I found that the students were familiar with other essays and books that I had written. They were keen to learn about the academic environments in America and Britain from someone like me, who had left Asia for Britain. After the question and answer session was finished, many of them at once came up to the podium, asking which universities were the best ones to study at, and whether they should think of going to America or to Britain.

After that my wife and I visited Sian and Shanghai. The reason for choosing Sian was that we wanted to see the city that had been so admired by Japanese in the past. It was indeed a beautiful, calm place. Before leaving Shanghai for Japan, we suddenly decided to visit Suzhou, not because we were attracted by the beauty and cultural heritage of the city (I am not that much of a cultured man), but because we wanted to ride on a Chinese train. On the way there we rode on the 'soft seats' (first class) of an ordinary train, and on the way back on the 'hard seats' (second class) of a special express. The cost of the special express ticket was more or less offset by the cost of the first class ticket, so there was hardly any difference in the price. It struck me that both trains were surprising modern compared to the North China Transport (Kahoku Kotsu) trains that I had ridden on over 50 years ago. Even by a fairly strict assessment, they were definitely superior to the special expresses that run on local lines in Japan.

At least as far as the various cities that I visited are concerned, I was not aware of the big gap in wealth between China and Japan shown in the statistics. In outward appearance the train which I boarded from Suzhou was very similar to the newest double decker train on Japan's Shinkansen (the *Nozomi*). While the seats were categorized as 'hard', it was not a case of sitting directly on wooden seats; they were more like second-class seats in Britain, or seats on underground trains. If one goes from Britain to America one is amazed at the abundance of foodstuffs, and at their low price, but in China also we were surprised at being able to eat cheaply and well, as long as we went to restaurants frequented by Chinese people, and not just those aimed at foreigners.

VII

The above are my impressions on visiting China in 1997. For the past four years I have visited Japan on an annual basis, spending about three months there each year. Comparing Japanese university students to those at Nankai University, I found a very great difference in the will to succeed of the two groups. (Nankai is China's third-best university, while the university that I went to in Japan did not hold that sort of status, so to compare them is perhaps not quite fair to Japan.) In Japan going to university is taken for granted, so becoming a university student is no great shakes, but in China going to university brings with it the promise of an élite career. The female student who most ably acted as interpreter when I gave my lectures in English was keen to study at Harvard, but switched to come instead to LSE, my own university. She has been in London since October, 1998. This alone suggests that my lectures were a success, and at the same time demonstrates the speed at which their decisions can be made. LSE has provided a scholarship for her.

In Japan 'élite' is not a word that carries with it good connotations. While Japanese people may be members of the élite, they very much dislike being referred to as such. Students therefore have no consciousness of themselves as an élite. However, since by the élite we mean the crack units who constitute the nucleus of society, any society which lacks an élite is a spineless society. I have often wondered whether this is a problem for Japan in comparing it with Britain, but felt it far more acutely when I visited China.

In China between 5 and 10 per cent of every year's birth cohort go on to university, probably somewhere around 6–7 per cent. In Japan, however, very large numbers go to university, so entering university brings with it no promise of becoming part of the nucleus of a future society. Thus Japanese people do not develop an élite awareness until they have joined a good company or government office, and have virtually reached the stage where they have been victorious in the competition for advancement and at last reached the higher echelons of that company or office. At this point they have long ceased to be people of any integrity. In order to be successful in that competition, many have earned their position through exploiting their own tact, and even using all sorts of dirty tricks. It is apparent that such an élite – even if it can be called by that name – does not possess the vitality to mobilize society.

This is absolutely clear if we compare the top Chinese politicians I have mentioned already, and politicians in Japan. Many of Japan's politicians are politicians' sons, who have inherited their political bases from their parents. Few of them applied their energies in their student days to any devotion to learning, so they are lacking in the ability to analyze things in a logical manner. Doubtless this group does include some who may have immersed themselves in sport, or played a focal part in club activities in pursuit of their hobbies. However, while individuals of this kind may well have a good understanding of people's feelings, they can hardly be said to possess the ability to think logically, so as politicians they are, in effect, damaged goods. Being good at factional struggles, and bringing factions together to choose a prime minister, are the sort of tricks that in Britain characterized the period when politics was operated by the so-called 'people of influence' two and a half centuries ago. Such a political crowd is absolutely no match for the politicians of China.

In the British case, to eradicate the evils resulting from the domination of politics by 'people of influence', political parties were formed as policy groupings. A system of electoral politics was established, with the choice between the policies of each party being entrusted to the people. In Japan the political parties, with the exception of the Communist Party, have never become policy groupings which present to the people policies agreed by party members, and seek election on that basis. In as far as public pledges are made in the context of an election, the vast majority are of the kind that involve serving the interests of the local electorate. Japan's first priority should not be the administrative reform of government bureaucracy, but reform of politics, to drive from the world of politics the second generation of people of influence who do not have what it takes to be a politician. If this is going to be entrusted to the politicians themselves, however, we might as well virtually give up all hope of reform, since not many politicians will be willing to contemplate their own destruction.

It is not surprising that the Japan Communist Party should be somewhat 'European'. Since Marx's ideas on communism were one strand of European thought, the structure of the party, too, is along European lines. The other Japanese parties, however, are flimsy edifices, lacking in any sense of modernity, so for a while the Japan Communist Party now needs to play an active role not as the party of communism, but as the party that can rectify Japan. The party must become the party of the Japanese people.

There is a great deal of opposition to communism among the Japanese people. In order to satisfy those people as well, the Communist Party needs to push for changes in Japanese politics. For that reason the party needs at least for a while to dispense with its professions of communism, and perhaps even drop the word 'communist' from its name. Such a change would be likely to make it easier to increase the party's influence. We must also remember that Marx, Engels and Lenin all stressed that modernization had to be the first priority, as the introduction of communism in a society controlled by people of influence was unlikely to be successful. This is obvious from their writings and essays.

If there is no wind, a sailing ship will not move. As long as there is some wind, whether fair or foul, a ship will be able to move forward, albeit slowly, but in a dead calm a ship will not move at all. It is the task of politicians to make the wind blow in society, by generating new ideas. The conservative wing of Japan's politicians does not possess the strength to do this. This is the reason why, despite being myself a radical liberal, I am placing my hopes for Japan on the Communist Party. If the Communist Party can grow into a national party, and negotiate with the other countries of northeast Asia to build together an Asian community, there will be the possibility of some movement occurring again in the region. But remember that such a Communist Party is not a party of communism at all. It is a party of all sensible liberal individuals for liberalism.

Lecture 1
The Hostile Relationship in Northeast Asia

This series of lectures consists of four talks. I am first going to try and explain the overall plan. The final objective of the lecture series as a whole is to substantiate the conclusion that it is essential for China, Taiwan, North and South Korea, and Japan to build in the future a cooperative community, as has been done by the countries of Europe. In the first lecture I will say something about past relations between these countries. There are both pluses and minuses in the history of these relationships, and I am going to start with the minus side, the history of war, and then in the second lecture say something about the positive side of relations, mainly the influence of Chinese thought and civilization on neighbouring countries. One of the topics in the second lecture will also be my thoughts on China's contemporary polity, and 'communism'.

The core issue will be raised in the last two lectures. The third lecture will be concerned with questions such as the exact nature of a nation state, whether any national polity is immutable, and whether the form of a nation state is likely to change in the light of technological change. In the fourth lecture I will present my ideas for a northeast Asian community. Whether or not the formation of an economic community will before long lead to political federation is a major question, as has become clear in the case of Europe. Such a question would arise in the case of Asia, too. My own belief is that such a federation will come into being in the distant future. We are, however, talking in this case about a future so distant that all or most of us present in this hall – I in my old age, the rest of you much younger – will be dead. When the future is that distant, people are apt to make irresponsible predictions.

Nevertheless, I do feel that providing technological development does not strengthen the destructive tendencies towards violence in our society, the world is likely to be brought together in a number of large federations, and it is these that will run the United Nations.

Whatever the case, the issues that I am going to talk about are both numerous and diverse. It is extremely difficult to discuss them in a coordinated and logically coherent manner; moreover, many of you will probably hold views very different from mine. I am sure that there will also be large numbers of you who have no interest in the very distant past. If we do not know how people lived in the past, however, we cannot make proposals about the future. In discussing difficult questions, we should as far as possible minimize the knowledge people are assumed to have, but we cannot know anything about the results of whether that was the right way to progress until the discussion is finished.

I

Talking about Japanese history is extremely difficult, especially for someone like me who was educated before the war. The history that we were taught began with stories which can only be regarded as absurd fabrications, starting with the deity Kuninotokotachi. It is likely that even the authors of the *Nihon Shoki* (720) and the *Kojiki* (712) regarded the age of the gods not as history but as legend. However, a primary or middle-school pupil before or during the war, knowing that after the start of the imperial period the first emperor had died at the age of 127, and that the first sixteen emperors had an average life span of 98 years, would probably also think that the early part of the imperial period could be counted as myth as well.[1] To think this way would be no more than healthy common sense.

In the case of China each dynasty wrote the history of the dynasty that had preceded it, so China left impartial and critical historical annals in which people could have some confidence. By contrast, in Japan both the *Nihon Shoki* (720) and the *Kojiki* (712) were compiled by imperial decree, and so they ended up as paeons to the imperial family, with little consideration given to the degree of objectivity of the historical evidence.[2] (The same can be said of company histories in contemporary Japan. The purpose of the history is to be self-congratulatory, and the materials are only there as support for this praise.)

Since the Second World War whatever is old has ended up as 'myth'. Having become 'myth', it ceased to be a matter of concern as to whether or not it really was. As 'myth', everything becomes truth. Thus the ancient history of the prewar period has continued to flourish in the postwar period in the form of myth. However, after the war there has been a substantial amount of land development accompanied by major public works, and this has resulted in the discovery of large numbers of burial mounds and other finds, leading to large scale archaeological excavations being carried out. These excavations have produced a large volume of material evidence relating to ancient times. As a result the origins of the state in the Japanese archipelago have gradually become clearer. Of course, it cannot yet be said that we know as much as we would like, but it is now possible tentatively to give a rough outline of what happened.

Contemporary historians believe that Japan's historical period can be traced back at least to the time of Empress Suiko at the end of the sixth century. This being the case, we can probably have some confidence in events as far back as the time of Emperor Keitai at the start of the sixth century. This is because Keitai was Empress Suiko's grandfather, and grandchildren tend to remember fairly clearly back as far as their grandparents. However, between Emperor Keitai and his predecessor, Buretsu, there was no direct blood-tie, and Keitai was made out to be the fifth-generation descendant of Emperor Ojin. He was, moreover, a resident not of Yamato, but of Fukui, around 100 kilometres away. On achieving the status of emperor, he at once headed for Yamato, but it was not until some 20 years later that he was able to establish his capital in Yamato. This means that for 20 years he was kept out of Yamato. On top of that, he had no connection with Emperor Ojin except for one which dated from around two centuries earlier. Between Emperor Keitai and Buretsu, there seems to have been a major discontinuance. At the end of Buretsu's reign there was either a civil war, in which Keitai seized power, or else Buretsu had no heir, so Keitai was invited to succeed him. However, in the latter case it would have been highly unusual for there to have been nobody suitable in the Yamato area, necessitating going as far as Fukui to search out a family related to the imperial family. The theory of a civil war seems rather more likely.

This being the case, it is probably better to regard the period from Jinmu to Buretsu as the Old Yamato dynasty, and that from Keitai onwards as the New Yamato dynasty. The emperors of the old dynasty were not well known to the writers of the *Nihon Shoki* and the *Kojiki*, so they just wrote nonsensical anecdotes about them, and they all ended up as emperors of a legendary age.[3]

By contrast, in the ancient Chinese annals Japan is referred to by a number of names, including Wa, the people of Wa, the country of Wa, Nihon, and the country of Nihon. In the ancient Tang annals, in which the country of Wa and Nihon appear side by side, we find written: 'The country of Nihon is separate from the country of Wa. Since that country is near to where the sun rises, it is referred to by the name of Nihon (lit. source of the sun). It is alternatively said that the country of Wa disliked its own name as being unrefined, and so renamed itself Nihon. It is also said that Nihon was formerly a small country, but it amalgamated with the territory of the country of Wa.' (*Kyutosho Wanokoku Nihonden* (revised edition, Iwanami Bunko, p. 90).

This means that one theory of what happened is that the country of Wa changed its name, while the other suggests that Nihon merged with the country of Wa. The first of these theories conforms with Japan's mythical ancient history, which claims that the country of Wa in Kyushu moved eastwards to establish the ancient Yamato dynasty, and at the same time renamed itself Nihon. The second explanation corresponds to the fact that after being defeated by the forces of the Tang Chinese and Silla at the battle of Paekson River in 622, the resources of the country of Wa were exhausted. It collapsed in 700 and became part of Nihon, which the following year established within the former country of Wa a government office (Dazaifu) to control the area. It is not necessarily impossible, however, for these two theories to coexist. This is because it is may be that one family from Kyushu (which may, or may not, have been one of the families within the country of Wa) moved to Yamato, and became the ruler of Yamato; then somewhat later this Yamato dynasty seized the country of Wa, which had been weakened in the wake of the conflict at the Paekson River.

As far as the *Kojiki* is concerned, there is virtually nothing on the battle at Paekson River. (The history dealt with by the *Kojiki* ends before the battle.) To write in detail about this would amount to a recognition of the existence of Wa, and to go in any depth into the relationship between Wa and the country of Nihon would mean acknowledging that the Japanese islands had been ruled by Wa before the country of

Nihon. The people of Nihon wiped out all traces of the existence of Wa, and it is thought that history was rewritten so that incidents which related to Wa appeared as incidents in the history of Nihon. The battle at Paekson River occurred at a time when both Wa and the country of Nihon were in existence. The conflict was at a time when Silla was attacking Paekche, and Wa, which had close contacts with Paekche, sent troops to help it, while the Tang were on the side of Silla. At Paekson River Wa was defeated by the joint forces of the Tang and Silla, and many people from Paekche fled to Wa. Help was also sought from Nihon.

Nihon also moved to intervene in the events. Emperor Saimei, accompanied by his Crown Prince, advanced with his troops as far as Chikushi in Kyushu, but then delayed for a long time in Kyushu. There is, however, no further record whatsoever of Nihon's crossing the sea and participating in the fighting. It seems likely that the elderly emperor and the imperial family had from the start no intention of joining the battle in Silla. All that is said in the *Kojiki* and *Nihon Shoki* is that two and a half months after the elderly emperor died at Chikushi the Crown Prince and his followers returned to Yamato. Since it is written in the Chinese *History of the Three Kingdoms* that it was the army of Wa that was defeated at the battle at Paekson River, we can probably conclude that the army of Nihon at the very most acted only as a rearguard, doing no more than advancing as far as Chikushi, and protecting the Wa stronghold, whose defence was weakened by the departure of its troops to the front. Nihon itself sustained virtually no damage from the conflict. Wa, by contrast, seems to have become impoverished by the expedition, losing its military strength as a result of the defeat, and subsequently collapsing, to be absorbed by Nihon.

There are, however, some difficulties in the idea of a peaceful takeover by the Yamato dynasty of the Kyushu dynasty. The Yamato dynasty at the time of the takeover was not the old dynasty of the mythical period that had moved east from Kyushu, but the dynasty founded by Keitai (the current emperor), whose relationship to the old dynasty is not clear. Even allowing for objective proof of a blood relationship between Emperor Keitai and the old dynasty, it is likely that the sentiments of Keitai's side towards members of the country of Wa in Kyushu were far from being those of a fraternal ally. Much more likely was a relationship being similar to that of conqueror and conquered. Moreover, if there was no blood relationship between the

Keitai party and the old Yamato dynasty, the relationship between the country of Wa and Nihon (Keitai dynasty) would have been no more than the relationship of strangers, underlining the statement in the Chinese histories that the countries of Nihon and Wa were separate entities.

That the relationship between Emperor Keitai and the country of Wa was far from amicable is also suggested by Keitai's attacking and defeating Iwai, king of Chikushi. This was clearly prior to Paekson River. It seems likely, therefore, that the Yamato army made a show of strength by stationing its troops in Chikushi, on the pretext of giving support when the forces of the country of Wa were depleted through the dispatch of troops to Paekson River, but that the troops were withdrawn as a result of the death of the emperor. Inadequacy of sources means that we cannot know exactly what took place, but it is clear that Nihon sustained almost no losses from the Paekson River conflict, and that Nihon afterwards closed its eyes to the outside world, concentrating its energies on honing its internal affairs.

What, then, can we say about the country of Wa? My own observations are drawn from Lee Byung Chu's two-volume *Kankoku Kodai Shi* (Ancient History of Korea) (Rokko Shuppan, 1979) and Furuta Takehiko's series of research works on ancient Japanese history. I have summarized these findings as follows in my own words as far as I think they are essential for the discussion below.

In ancient times there were remarkably close ties between northern Kyushu (the country of Wa) and southern Korea, that is, the group of small principalities centred around Mimana. Even today it is not impossible to cross the straits to Korea in a small boat, but it is thought that in ancient times, when small boats were the only means of transport available, seafaring peoples were able to manoeuvre their small craft with a remarkable degree of efficiency. Since in the distant past the Korean peninsula and the Japanese islands had been joined to each other, and the Japan Sea had been an inland sea, at the time of the country of Wa there may have been other islands which could act as a staging post apart from Iki and Tsushima. The people of Mimana probably lived in Wa as well, and vice versa. There was, of course, intermarriage between the two peoples.

At that time Mimana, with its land connection with China, was overwhelmingly superior in cultural terms. Given its associations with Mimana, the cultural level of Wa was in its turn far higher than those of the other kingdoms on the Japanese islands, and it was Wa that started to use writing first, substantially before the Yamato dynasty acquired a knowledge of Chinese characters. From a Korean perspective those areas of the Japanese archipelago outside northern Kyushu were all barbarian territories, and great possibilities were thought to exist in such barbarian territories because they were so unexploited. Relations between Korea and Japan at that time somewhat resembled those between Britain and America after the discovery of North America by Columbus, when the English Puritans emigrated there.

Just as the rate of growth of America was higher than that of Britain, so, during the period from the third to fourth centuries through to the tenth and eleventh centuries, did the rate of growth of Japan far outstrip that of Korea. After the eighth century Japan was no longer the country of Wa, but the new Yamato dynasty, that of Keitai, which had absorbed the country of Wa. The old Tang records write of them, 'the visitors from that country are extremely arrogant, they do not answer with sincerity, and so the Chinese people are suspicious of them'. Japan is a country that has from ancient times grown rapidly through the effective use of the flow of culture from other countries, and the people of such countries usually tend to be arrogant as a counter of their own inferiority. Moreover, such an attitude of bravado was naturally despised by China and Korea, which had been the source of that culture; they were cautious about believing what the Japanese said about Japan.

The passage through Wa (now Hakata) was not the only route from Korea. There were also routes through Karatsu, Izumo, Wakasa and Echizen. Of these, Keitai came from Echizen. It is perfectly possible that his own ancestors, or those of his family, had come from Korea, and he could have made skilful use of arrivals from there. Echizen was, moreover, an area that produced iron. It is not hard to imagine how the advanced iron-producing technology of Korea was used to make iron goods, facilitating the production of weapons and the development of more advanced methods of agriculture, resulting in the accumulation of overwhelming wealth. Keitai and his family advanced south into Yamato, and succeeded the old Yamato dynasty that was said to have been founded by Jinmu in his movement towards the east from the Wa area. (Recent archaeological findings seem more or less to have confirmed the existence of this old Yamato dynasty as being something of very ancient origin.)

So, there were very close ties between Japan and Korea, as shown above. The result was that the Japanese people ended up being very different from the people of Korea – just as the people of America are quite different in character from the British. The Japanese were regarded from early on as being arrogant. While this was one aspect of the sense of inferiority towards Korea and China at the time when the country was founded, this arrogant attitude, which led to Japanese claims of superiority to Korea and China, remained even after they had become more confident in themselves. It became irredeemable.

II

In the time of the Mongols China invaded Japan. In 1274 and 1281 there were attempts to attack Fukuoka in northern Kyushu (the location of the original capital of Wa), and some of the forces landed, but on each occasion there occurred a violent storm, the invading army lost its ships and was defeated. (The violent storms on these occasions were thought to have been caused by the gods for the protection of Japan, and so were called *kamikaze* – divine wind. This is the origin of what were later known as the *kamikaze* corps of the Japanese army.) Both in the case of Paekson River, and in the case of the attacks on Kyushu, the invading forces were defeated.

Leaving aside the 15-year conflict between China and Japan in this century, other major conflicts in Asia since the time of the Mongols include the Korean invasion carried out by Toyotomi Hideyoshi. Fighting took place on two occasions, in 1592 and 1597, and in both cases the Japanese forces were ultimately defeated in the vicinity of Seoul by combined Ming (Chinese) and Korean troops. War is said to be a means to an end, but it is not clear in the case of either of these conflicts exactly what the objective was. They seem to have been wars without reason.

In as far as there was a reason, it seems to have been a war aimed at eradicating Christianity, as stated by James Murdoch. Hideyoshi was aware that the military forces of the Christian *daimyo* (lords) were both brave and strong. He therefore mobilized them to invade Korea. Should they be defeated, the forces of the Christian *daimyo* would have been wiped out, something that Hideyoshi greatly desired. Should they be victorious, and succeed in occupying Korea, their achievements could be rewarded by grants of land in Korea, which would effectively have driven them from Japan to Korea. This outcome, too, would not have been a bad one for Hideyoshi. Since he would have been satisfied whatever the outcome, it was a rational measure for Hideyoshi to send an invasion force to Korea. If pressed, we could say that it was an imperialistic war to seize territory for one's followers. The result of this 'rational war', however, was to plant in the minds of Koreans a thoroughgoing suspicion of Japan.

After that there was no major conflict in northeast Asia up until the war between China and Japan in 1894–95. This was because during the Tokugawa period an isolationist policy was pursued. Isolationism had three major results. Firstly, it almost wiped out the Christian *daimyo*. Secondly, it facilitated total control over the import of weapons. Thirdly, given that Hideyoshi's second invasion of Korea was the result of conflict over which of them had been victorious on the occasion of the first invasion, it prevented a third invasion of Korea by freezing diplomatic relations between the two countries.

Therefore the Meiji government's reopening of Japan was accompanied by disputes with China. From the time of its foundation, Japan had up to that point always striven to 'catch up and overtake', trying to catch up not the countries of the West, but China. Japan achieved victory over China in 1895. Why the one had been victorious, and the other defeated, was given a great deal of consideration in both countries. The answer that was given was the same in both. In China outstanding individuals were selected by the traditional examination system to be civil rather than military officials. However, as a result of the status system in Japan members of the military class also took administrative posts, and civilians were looked down upon. This conclusion led in China to calls for the revision or abolition of the examination system, and in Japan to a situation where even the Prime Minster could not speak out on issues relating to the supreme command of the armed forces. Civilian control of the military became impossible in Japan.

This is not enough by itself, however, to explain Japan's aggression in China from 1931. First of all, Japan's army was a conscript army. This meant that any war which did not have the support of the people could not be prosecuted over a lengthy period. Of course, fierce pressure could probably be put on dissidents, but before that point could be reached public opinion had to be unified to reduce the number of dissidents to a minority. My own view is that what united

Japan was the racism of the Japanese people. Up until the end of the Second World War not just the Japanese, but Europeans and Anglo-Americans as well were all racist. Japanese racism, however, was somewhat complex. On the one hand the Japanese discriminated against Chinese, Koreans and Taiwanese, and even more against other non-white peoples. On the other hand Japanese racism was characterized by reverse discrimination in relation to Caucasians, that is to say, the Japanese bore a grudge against Caucasians, who, they believed, discriminated against them. This hatred of white people played an important role in the Second World War.

It is clear that racism, in the form of feelings of contempt for non-white peoples, was also deep rooted in Western countries. Western feelings in relation to Japan, however, were of a particular kind, comprising a mixture of contempt and at the same time fear at the speed with which Japan seemed to be gaining on their position. The circumstances were regarded as conferring upon the Japanese people in general a sense of destiny, something often referred to at the time as the world destiny of the Japanese people. This destiny of the Japanese was to eliminate the discrimination that existed between the West and Japan, and to put Japan on an equal footing with the West. Achieving this would also be of immense significance for the history of the world, in that it would have the additional benefit of enhancing the status of other non-white peoples. Since the Japanese themselves, however, discriminated against non-white peoples, they had no desire whatsoever to see the end of such discrimination. What the Japanese wanted was a hierarchical system of races, in which they themselves were at the apex of the non-white races, and on an equal footing with Caucasians, but with the various peoples of Asia subordinate to Japan, and the other non-white peoples even lower down the hierarchy. This was the kind of system that was meant when Japan was talked of as 'the leader of Asia'. In other words, only the Japanese could become honorary whites.

III

However, such an atmosphere or trend in public opinion was again not enough by itself to cause a war. Moreover, since the Japanese regarded war as a race war against almost all white people, the general jingoism of the Japanese people would not by itself have led to war. What is critical in this kind of situation is the attitude of politicians and of the military. There had existed for a while in Japan a number of politicians and politically minded members of the military who were inclined to provoke a conflict with a view to making Japan the 'leader of Asia' should a favourable opportunity arise. It is difficult to know, however, what sort of circumstances they may have regarded as being favourable for the initiation of a conflict, and very hard to explain why Japan ignited the fuse of war at that particular moment. Let us therefore start with a bit of history.

The year 1887 was only 20 years after the Meiji Restoration, and at that time Japan was clearly still behind China. In that year Tani Tateki, who had rendered distinguished service in the Restoration, presented a statement of his opinions, in which he wrote:

> Sooner or later the time must come when Europe will erupt into conflict and be trampled underfoot by the warring parties. Although our country should initially not become involved in any European upheaval, the ramifications of such an upheaval will be very extensive, so it is almost certain that it will bring unrest to the East, and provoke upheaval there as well. Therefore if our country is able to achieve the position of leader among all the countries of the East, rather than thinking about its importance in relation to the countries of the West, and if at that time our country can muster twenty durable warships and 100,000 picked troops, this will be a demonstration to the Western powers that Japan can hold its own as their rival in the East.[4]

Kita Ikki, who wielded enormous influence over young army officers in the late 1920s and early 1930s, made similar pronouncements.

Such statements by Tani and others were an indication of Japan's subsequent path, with its defeat of China, its annexation of Korea, the establishment of empire in Manchuria, and the deployment of Japanese troops right across China. This course of action was founded on the arrogance identified in the ancient Tang annals, amplified in a complex manner as a result of the Japanese people's new experience of an inferiority complex towards the West prior to the Meiji Restoration. Towards the end of the Tokugawa period all the countries of northeast Asia – China, Korea and Japan – were at a loss to know whether to try and expel these barbarians, or whether to open their doors. In the case of Japan, both the *Bakufu* officials responsible for the diplomatic question, and the domain loyalists, initially agreed to have as their overriding policy the continuation of isolation. They were prepared to go to war with the Western European powers if that were necessary to achieve this objective. However, first of all the *Bakufu* was compelled to agree to open the country. Then conflicts with the West brought home to Satsuma and Choshu as well that a policy of expelling the barbarians was just not feasible.

The result of all this was that Japan became committed to opening up the country, but this was not because Japan was convinced of the need for the trading and cultural interchange that came with the opening of the country. In consequence, while Japan embarked on a period during which it was forced to open up the country, this did not mean that the Japanese discarded their ideas of expelling the barbarians. They retained attitudes that could very easily become anti-foreign. As Tani had predicted, there was before long a major upheaval in Europe, but the first time round, by being on the Anglo-French side, Japan had little opportunity to take advantage of the resultant instability in Asia, and become at a stroke the leader of the East. The second time that war broke out in Europe, however, the country attempted to take advantage of the confusion and place the whole of the East at a stroke under Japanese domination, exactly as Tani had advocated. The traditional inferiority complex of the Japanese people was reduced to an excessive delusion of persecution, resulting in an upsurge of national awareness, and jingoistic and imperialistic sentiments among the Japanese people.

There were also unscrupulous criminals about. Japan's imperialist aggression, whether on the occasion of the annexation of Korea, or at the time of the Manchurian Incident and the war against China, was a contemptible performance, for which Japan alone was responsible.[5] Moreover in all of these cases Japan, unchanged from the view expressed in the ancient Tang annals, had no compunction about lying, and failed to respond with sincerity. Since it was a question of one's country first, individual achievement advanced in accordance with the predicted scenario, with the result that anything was acceptable as long as Japan was successful in her aggression. In as far as they shared equally in the spoils that were seized, these deserving retainers and generals got fat on aggression. They provoked incidents with the express purpose of gain.

On one occasion only were they unsuccessful. In the closing stages of the First World War France and Britain called upon Japan to send troops into Siberia. This stemmed from concerns that victory for the Bolshevik faction in the Russian revolution might lead to the conclusion of a peace treaty between Russia and Germany, which might in turn mean that German forces from the Eastern Front were thrown into the Western Front, increasing the pressure on France and Britain. To try and forestall this happening France and Britain requested Japan to send troops to Siberia in support of the White Russian forces. There was division within Japan over what policy to pursue, with the Foreign Ministry opposed to sending troops, and the army in favour, but ultimately the Foreign Ministry gave way, agreeing that if America were to send troops Japan would have no alternative but to act similarly. This led to Japan sending in troops along with the United States, but the war in Europe ended only three months later.

France and Britain, who both regarded the dispatch of troops as having achieved its objective, now demanded that the troops be withdrawn from Siberia. The United States immediately withdrew its forces on the entirely appropriate grounds that since US forces had joined the expedition with a view to securing the surrender of Germany, it was not proper to keep them there now that that objective had been achieved. The Japanese army, however, tormented by its complex towards the West, could not comprehend this logic, and it adjudged the demand for rapid withdrawal of troops so soon after their dispatch as nothing more than Western European selfishness. Japan did not find it easy to withdraw her troops, with the last units being brought back only in 1925, seven years after the end of the Great War.

The Siberian expedition, unlike the Sino-Japanese and Russo-Japanese wars, brought Japan neither new territory nor any indemnity. The self-interest of the generals went unsatisfied, and they fuelled the theories of European selfishness. As a reaction to the withdrawal, the army afterwards became more and more radical, and looked for booty not from the West or Russia, but from within Asia itself.

There was something else as well. Before the Meiji Restoration Japan had moved towards opening the country, and concluded unequal treaties with a number of Western countries. These unequal treaties were a source of shame, as they neither allowed Japan tariff autonomy, nor police authority in the concessions around the open ports. The Meiji government focused its attention on replacing these treaties by more equal ones, but it was not until 1911, over 50 years after the treaties were first concluded, that they were successful in regaining tariff autonomy. (Treaty revision and abolition of the foreign settlements were agreed in 1894.) The damage that this inequitable tariff system did to the Japanese economy was more than largely nominal. A low wage system, for example, was unavoidable if Japan were to surmount the tariff disadvantage and compete successfully with Western commodities. The unequal treaties fostered resentment of whites among the Japanese people, and were the source of 'reverse discrimination' against Europeans.[6]

Hatred of the Caucasian countries was further inflamed by the failure to agree to Japan's call at the Versailles Peace Conference for the inclusion of a racial equality clause in the charter of the League of Nations. Then at the Washington Conference (1921–22) Japanese naval strength was limited to a lower level than that of Britain and the United States, and it was decided that the rights and interests Japan had obtained in Shandong during the First World War should be returned. The Anglo-Japanese Alliance was also abandoned. This chain of events implanted in the minds of Japanese a fundamental suspicion of the West, and at the same time instilled into them a highly jingoistic sense of nation. These sentiments, moreover, became ever more exaggerated as a rival spiritual response to the democracy, pacifism and inter-nationalism that were being advocated at the same time. On top of that Japan demanded that the various countries of Asia enter into the same unequal relationship with Japan that Japan itself had experienced. The racial equality that Japan had in mind at this time was not true equality, but a racial inequality that allowed for discrimination between Japanese and other non-white peoples. When the Japanese spoke of becoming the leader of the East such a relationship of inequality with the rest of Asia was not merely implied, but expected.

This 'imperialism' on the part of Japan was not imperialism in the sense of Marx, Lenin and Sweezy. Japan's imperialism did not emerge at the stage of monopoly capitalism, the highest stage of capitalism as indicated by Marx. Japan was already initiating overseas aggression when her capitalist economy was still in its infancy and youth. However, it was imperialism in the broad sense that Schumpeter had conceived of it. The state had an unlimited desire for expansion, just as in the case of the ancient Roman empire and modern European autocratic monarchs, and this desire ended up with the military control of other countries. Aggression of this kind was more the product of an irrational, pre-capitalist stage of development, and made it difficult in its turn for the country to reach a capitalist stage, at which the state could become more of a *Gesellschaft* (society of interest), and in which individuals could be autonomous and stand up for their rights. Japanese believe that Japan participated in aggression because Japan had modernized, but the aggression occurred because Japan was premodern.

In the case of Japan it was not just that the Japanese had always been arrogant, but that the country had been compelled by more advanced countries to swallow the bitter pill of the unequal treaties and the withdrawal at the end of the Siberian expedition. This had sent people into a frenzy of rage. There was no question of capitalism reaching to an advanced stage, as stated by the Marxists. In Korea the advance of Japan's modern industries did not occur until some time after the annexation, and in Manchuria as well the great *zaibatsu* enterprises were initially hesitant about becoming involved there. Apart from the large enterprises associated with the government, there existed in Manchuria the Manchurian Heavy Industries Corporation (Nissan) and some other large enterprises, but none of them, including Nissan, had ventured into Manchuria because they were large enterprises. They seem to have become large enterprises (or the Manchurian Heavy Industries Corporation) because they ventured into Manchuria.

This kind of premodern imperialism was far more brutal than the imperialism of Marx and Lenin, and ended up enslaving the peoples of the countries that were defeated. The ringleaders of the aggression were the army and the right wing, but neither the Emperor, nor the capitalists or businessmen had the courage to try and check them. Instead they merely confirmed the actions of the ringleaders. Through this confirmation their aggression ultimately came to be carried out in the name of the emperor.

Many of the ringleaders were members of families who had held the highest rank of the warrior class under the Tokugawa status system prior to the Restoration, but after the Restoration the status of these families, except for that of the generals and admirals, had declined. The Restoration was a time of drastic upheaval, and those who lost out as a result continued to feel that they could promote their own interests through aggression against foreign countries. Some branches of the government and the army hatched plots in accordance with this objective; those involved in these plots were totally lacking in idealism, in considered thought, and in international awareness. Ideological slogans such as 'liberating the peoples of the East from the Caucasians' and 'eight corners of the world under one roof' were, as we have already seen, rooted in racial prejudice, and were no more than slogans brandished by one segment of the intelligentsia under the leadership of the military at a time when Japan had become bogged down in the war against China.

The annexation of Korea, the Manchurian Incident and the war against China were all conducted in a manner guaranteed to stir up feelings of hatred for Japan among the peoples of Korea and China. Korea, first of all, was under the suzerainty of China, but other powers, including both Russia and Japan, sought to advance their interests there. The Korean Queen, Min, who was a member of the pro-Russian faction, became the victim of an assassination plot hatched by the Japanese envoy Miura Goro (a former soldier). The Japanese tried to claim that she had been killed as part of the struggle for power among the Koreans themselves, but foreigners who had witnessed the event testified to the fact that the deed had been carried out by Japanese.

Even before the Manchurian Incident there was a similar assassination, when the leading Manchurian warlord, Zhang Zuolin, was killed when the train on which he was travelling was blown up, following his failure to go along with what Japan wanted. The assassination was planned and implemented by Komoto Daisaku of the Guandong Army (Kantogun) staff, but the government claimed that the deed had been carried out by the Chinese. The Manchurian Incident, too, was initiated by a similar plot. The Guandong Army itself set off an explosion on the Japanese-owned South Manchurian Railway, making it look like something carried out by the Chinese, and then launched an attack on the Chinese Army under the guise of self-defence. The early phase of the war between China and Japan (the so-called China Incident) took the following course. Japan initiated hostilities on the grounds that Chinese troops had fired on Japanese troops engaged in manoeuvres in the vicinity of the Marco Polo Bridge, and it remains unclear even now whether this was the Japanese army's usual practice of carrying out these things itself, or whether the shots were fired by the Eighth Route Army (the troops of the Chinese Communist Party) with the aim of provoking the Japanese.

As for the Marco Polo Bridge Incident, at least as far as documents that can be obtained in Japan are concerned, judgment has to some extent to be withheld on the grounds that the matter is 'currently still under investigation', but a common thread runs consistently through the other incidents mentioned above. First, these incidents were all engineered by regular officials of the Japanese government, whether diplomats or soldiers of the Guandong Army. Secondly, it is notable that in each case a fabricated story that the incident had been perpetrated by the other side (whether Koreans or Chinese) was used as a pretext for opening fire on them. Repeated occurrences of this kind were bound to result in mistrust of the Japanese government by other countries. The Japanese government (cabinet and Emperor) failed to punish with any severity the plotters and perpetrators of these incidents, and, what was worse, ratified them and allowed them to escalate.

Since incidents of this kind violated the imperial prerogative, the perpetrators should have been subject to the harshest penalties for showing defiance of the Emperor, but because the Emperor, too, eventually ratified their actions, he, along with the cabinet of the time, must bear some responsibility for these incidents. Large forces became involved in an attempt to find a solution, and large numbers of people died.

IV

In this 'Emperor-system state' the order of the Emperor was sacred and inviolable, so the people were unable to resist, dying for and because of the Emperor. As we shall see below in Section VI, the people had no self-awareness, and hence made no claim to freedom, suffering themselves to be dragged along by the carriage of imperial power, just as Hegel had stated.

Under this Emperor-system state people had virtually no human rights. Because they themselves were like this, most Japanese believed that the Koreans and the Chinese, too, possessed no human rights. Thought about in this way, the massacre at Nanjing, the killings at Singapore and the use of women from Korea and other Asian countries as prostitutes for Japanese soldiers seemed totally explainable, things which would not have taken on much importance for the Japanese. Japan's soldiers and sailors killed the peoples of the colonies and occupied territories, or forced them into prostitution, in the spirit that anything done in the name of the Emperor was acceptable. In Japan under the Emperor system the people's ethical sense was paralyzed.

Of course the Koreans' and Chinese spirit of opposition and resistance to Japan gradually became stronger and stronger. America and Britain sent arms and ammunition to China, and volunteer troops to support the Chinese. The war was a long drawn out affair, with Japan becoming more and more embroiled. Japan started her southern advance with the aim of striking at China's supply routes.

At the time Hitler had already started the war in Europe. France had been overrun by the Germans, and it was the time of Hitler's puppet regime at Vichy. Japan negotiated with the Vichy regime with a view to obtaining agreement to Japan's advance into French Indo-China (Vietnam), and this was achieved. A few years before, Kita Ikki had been calling for policies similar policies to those advocated by Tani in his earlier statement, and Japan advanced southwards with a view to benefiting from the disruption in Europe, just as they had suggested, and attempted to cut off China's routes of supply. South and Southeast Asia at this time consisted of American, Dutch, and British colonies, and these countries joined China in imposing an economic embargo on Japan. They stated that the embargo would not be lifted unless Japan withdrew its troops from Vietnam and China. It was felt that if Japan were to refuse to comply with this demand, and the embargo was implemented, then Japan would be unable successfully to prosecute the war with China due to a lack of raw materials, and the Japanese army would ultimately under those circumstances have to withdraw from China. Whatever happened, Japan would have to withdraw one way or another.

The economic embargo was implemented when the Japanese army had already advanced into southern Vietnam. The Japanese government responded by bringing into effect its right of self-defence, but an economic embargo seems an obvious measure by today's common sense. We can only surmise how far a withdrawal on the part of the Japanese would have brought reconciliation with China and the lifting of the embargo, but under such circumstances Manchuria might well have remained in the hands of the Japanese. It is likely that Korea and Taiwan would almost certainly have remained under Japanese control. As for whether it would have been better for later Japanese had the Emperor system thus continued in Japan, or, as ultimately happened, for Japan to be defeated in war, to have lost these occupied territories and colonies, and for the Emperor system to be destroyed as well, over the long term it is certainly the second of these two options that is the better. However, at the time neither the Emperor, nor the ruling élite nor the army had the courage to adopt the withdrawal strategy. Fearing that internal conflict would be the result of withdrawal, they took the option of advancing to the south, a policy that in effect amounted to the suicide of the Emperor system.[7]

It was at this stage that slogans such as 'Greater East Asia Co-Prosperity Sphere', 'all the corners of the world under one roof', and 'liberating East Asia from the domination of the Caucasians' appeared. The Japanese government then rushed towards hostilities with Britain and the United States, in effect initiating the self-destruction of the Emperor system state. This decision on the part of the government was not the result of a will on the part of Japan to risk its own safety to try and liberate Asia from white control. If Japan had withdrawn from China in compliance with the demands made by China, America, Britain and Holland, the army would have completely lost face, undermining its position within the country. The army therefore jeopardized the safety of the whole country in order to protect its own position. This decision was made at an imperial conference in the presence of the Emperor.

At this conference the Emperor ought to have rejected the demands of the military. The Emperor does appear to have stated his desire for peaceful coexistence with other countries, but his opponents were hardly of the kind to retreat purely on the basis of such a gently worded suggestion. What he should have done, therefore, was to adopt a resolute attitude, which he did, in fact, do at the imperial conference at the time of Japan's defeat. The reason for the decision to initiate this great war, in which several million Japanese were to die, was thus the obscure one of 'self-preservation', which was not really a proper reason at all. What a blunder!

This meant that the ruling élite, which had continued to confirm the criminal actions carried out by some of its branch offices, without any approbation of the proper authorities, was now making its decisions in the presence of the Emperor himself, in an attempt to purge itself of its accumulated culpability. It has been emphasized after the war that as an individual the Emperor was a pacifist, and strongly disliked conflict, but this fact can never lessen the significance of the fact that the declaration of war was made on the basis of an imperial decision.

At that time, moreover, four years had already passed since the Marco Polo Bridge Incident, and ten years since the Manchurian Incident. During these years large numbers had died in the conflict, and the Japanese people were anxious for the war to end as soon as possible. These circumstances were disregarded by the Emperor and the government. Since the people possessed few rights, they had little choice but to go along with the imperial will. Surprisingly they did not follow the Emperor reluctantly. Many of them welcomed the war in a frenzy of joy.

This was because the slogan 'liberating Asia from Caucasian control' genuinely appealed to people, unlike the unrealistic slogan 'all the eight corners of the world under one roof'. The Japanese had a strong sense of grudge at, for example, the unequal treaties that Japan had been subjected to from the late Tokugawa period through to the late Meiji period, and the 'selfishness' of French and British demands for troop withdrawal on the occasion of the Siberian Expedition. Feelings of hatred based on a general inferiority complex towards Europe and the United States caused the Japanese to lose their reason, and to pledge themselves to 'die for the Emperor'.

The core of the pro-war party at the time, however, was the armed forces (particularly the army) and the right wing. The military officers had been trained to believe in the utmost importance of making their way in the world. While the essence of the military creed was service with loyalty, a conviction that a soldier who served with loyalty would rise in the world, while one who did not would not enjoy such success, meant that loyalty was equated with success. Advancement thus came to be regarded as the essence of being a soldier. For a soldier the most rapid route to advancement was war, and so the bands of loyalists who made up the armed forces were inevitably jingoistic. By contrast, the so-called patriots of the right wing were uninterested in personal advancement. However, since the core of this patriotic camp was made up of jingoistic members of the military, the right wing, too, was bound to be jingoistic. Thus the right-wing newspaper and book publishing companies stirred up the sentiments of war. Even the Emperor's response to those members of the military who had disrupted the chain of command and acted in contravention of their superiors, was to reward their 'meritorious services' with the Order of the Golden Kite in recognition of the results of their actions. The net effect was that the Emperor himself encouraged such insubordinate behaviour.

Such was the chaotic political environment of the early Showa period. Events culminated in the onset of the Pacific War, but the Japanese had little confidence and little prospect that fighting fairly and squarely would bring Japan victory. This was why a surprise attack was thought necessary. It was also apparent from the start that sooner or later the war would have to be brought to an end by diplomatic negotiation. It is inconceivable that the incompetent Japanese government which could not have found a solution to the war with China can make peace negotiations with America and Britain, since Japan has become ever weaker. Despite this the Emperor's government made the rash decision to start the war, and the reason why this was possible was that the Japanese people were unable to stand up for their liberties, and had been granted no human rights. The decision to go for war was made by the Emperor, the cabinet and the leadership of the armed forces in total disregard of the will of the people. Even so, the people rejoiced at the prospect of dying in the service of the Emperor, and were intoxicated with the thought of national self-genocide.

On the other hand, each British or American citizen made up his or her own mind freely as an individual, so it was extremely difficult for any kind of national consensus to be reached. Herein lies the key difference between the 'Emperor system state' of Japan, and what might be called a 'liberalist, democratic state'. The Japanese government regarded this situation as being advantageous to Japan, but the effect of Japan's lawless activities was to anger the American people, making it easy for a consensus of national opinion to be reached. The secretive attack on Pearl Harbor served only to harden conclusively the resolve of the American people for war.

There are some Japanese today who contend that the Pacific War was a war fought in self-defence, or a war for the liberation of Asia, but my own view is that such claims are totally mistaken. It was, to put it bluntly, an aggressive war typical of the latecomer imperialist country. At the time when the China War, and then the Pacific War, broke out, there already had existed in the countries invaded by Japan resistance movements against the earlier imperial powers, led by nationalists or communists. Many of the members of these movements had been arrested and imprisoned, or had gone underground. While the

Japanese army in fact came in as a new army of invasion, Japanese forces were initially welcomed by these nationalists and communists as being part of an army of liberation. This was analogous to Japan's communists' later misunderstanding of the role of the American Occupation forces. However, the true nature of the situation soon became apparent. They realized that the Japanese army perpetrated acts of extreme violence and brutality, and was certainly not a liberation army. There was a split between the nationalists and the communists. One side cooperated with the Japanese on the basis that one evil had to be counteracted with another, while the other chose the path of resistance to Japan, even if it meant allying themselves with the earlier imperialist powers. In order to ally themselves with the former group, i.e. the collaborationists, the Japanese brandished the ideological flag of the 'Greater East Asia Co-Prosperity Sphere' and 'Asian liberation', but it was already too late to do this. In every territory Japan was being defeated by the early imperialist countries.

Slogans of this kind were, moreover, fraudulent.[8] Asian liberation depended on Japan's being defeated, and should Japan be victorious Japanese rule would be maintained with Japan as the new hegemon of Asia. Asia could therefore not be liberated by Japan. Liberation could ultimately only be achieved over a long period by the nationalist and communist resistance movements against both the first and second generation of imperialist powers. Nor was the war we are talking about a war fought by Japan in self-defence. As already noted, even if Japan had withdrawn from China, Japan would not only have been able to retain intact all the proper territory of the so-called Greater Japanese Empire, but would very likely have been able to maintain Japanese influence over Korea and the Manchurian Empire as well. A withdrawal strategy could therefore be regarded as defending Japan's interests, obviating any need for a war of self-defence. It is thus apparent that the Pacific War was neither a war of liberation nor a war of self-defence. If this is the case, what, then, was the war actually fought for?

Clearly it was to preserve the Emperor system that the conflict was waged. This is apparent from the stated condition in the Japanese acceptance of surrender at the end of the war of 'preservation of the national polity (*kokutai*)'. Had Japan earlier on given in to the United States and Britain, and withdrawn her troops from China, it is likely that the higher echelons of government and the leadership of the army would have lost face, and as circumstances changed the Emperor system would probably have collapsed from within. This was something that was particularly feared by the military leadership, and Japan fought to preserve the Emperor system. Despite this the end of the war brought not just ruins, but the collapse of the Emperor system as well. This is because in contemporary democratized Japan the Emperor has lost almost all his political powers, remaining no more than a symbolic figure permitted to be involved in only a very limited number of matters of state.

V

Who, then, must bear responsibility for this war? Let me first of all outline the changes in the leadership of the main belligerents during the war period. In Asia the war commenced in 1931, in Europe in 1939. America was drawn in to these separate wars as a result of the attack on Pearl Harbor in 1941, which led to their fusion into a world war. To start with Europe, Germany and Italy were during this period fighting under the leadership of Hitler and Mussolini respectively. America, too, fought the war virtually under the leadership of one man, Roosevelt, up until the time of his death in 1945. (On Roosevelt's death he was succeeded by Vice-President Truman, who was in charge for the last few months of the war.)

There was some resemblance between the constitutional monarchy system of Britain and the Emperor system of Japan. This was the time of King George VI in Britain, and of Emperor Hirohito in Japan. There was some difference in the political roles and powers of the king and the emperor, but both monarchs were the formal repository of political decision-making. The actual content of such decision-making, however, was in both cases determined by the prime minister and his Cabinet members. For that reason political responsibility resided with the cabinet. In the case of Japan, however, it is unclear whether or not the emperor could be held responsible.

Nevertheless, there was one marked difference between the two countries. The British prime minister at the start of the European war was Chamberlain. Chamberlain, however, was blamed for failing to halt the German invasion of Norway in the early months of the war, and resigned, handing over power to Churchill in May, 1940. Churchill remained in charge of the war effort right through the German surrender and afterwards, until just before the surrender of

Japan. In Britain, therefore, it was Churchill who was the major architect of victory.

Japan, by contrast, had no fewer than 14 prime ministers during the 14-year period from the start of the Manchurian Incident in September, 1931, up until Japan's defeat in the Pacific War in August, 1945. The longest terms as prime minister were those of Tojo, who served 2 years 9 months, and Konoe during his first term of office, which lasted 2 years 7 months (even if his second and third terms are included, Konoe only served a total of 3 years 7 months as prime minister). Nevertheless, since Tojo served for a time as Army Minister in Konoe's cabinet, the two periods can be thought of together as the Konoe–Tojo years. However, since it was the two men's difference of opinion regarding how the China war should be brought to a conclusion that led to the fall of Konoe's cabinet, it is not tenable to argue that the two men were part of a common conspiracy to provoke war in the Pacific.

If we look at things in a bit more detail, we find that the 14 years of conflict with China and the Pacific War can be divided into three sub-periods. The first is that up until the 26 February Incident in 1936, during which time there were three prime ministers: Inukai, Saito and Okada. These men cannot under any circumstances be regarded as right wing or jingoistic, and it is not possible to assign to them any responsibility for the prolongation of the China conflict which subsequently lengthened into the Pacific War.

The second period is that from the time of the 26 February Incident up until the resignation of Konoe's third cabinet in October 1941. During these years there were no fewer than eight prime ministers. These were the years when the China war flared up again in 1937 with the so-called North China Incident, and the progressive spread of the conflict into the central and southern parts of the Chinese mainland, and into the country's hinterland. Then in September, 1940, Japan advanced troops into the northern part of French Indo-China. Efforts were also made during these years to bring Japan closer to Germany and Italy. In 1936 the Anti-Comintern Pact was concluded with Germany, and in 1940 a military alliance with the Axis powers of Germany and Italy. The attack on Pearl Harbor, therefore, did not just start the Pacific War. By bringing about a fusion of the Pacific and European conflicts, it plunged the whole world into a major war. However, Japan's motives for starting the war were concealed not just from its enemies (America, Britain and the other allies), but from its alliance partners (Germany and Italy) as well.

During these years preparations for war were also steadily advanced. One aspect of this preparation was control of the economy and the provision of expanded production facilities for munitions. Another was the attempt to impose unity on national opinion. Heterodox thought was eliminated or suppressed, and freedom of thought and belief ceased to exist altogether. This was a crucial preparatory period for the circumstances of the war, but the choice of successive prime ministers was lacking in any logical connection, pandering only to thoughts of short-term popularity. Apart from Konoe himself, the longest term of office was that of Hirota (less than 11 months), and the remainder all served for under eight months. The shortest of these cabinets was that of Hayashi, at four months, and it was Hayashi who, as commander of Japanese forces in Korea at the time of the Manchurian Incident, despatched troops across the border from Korea into Manchuria without an imperial decree. This was, of course, as illegal act that should have been punished through a court martial, but not only was Hayashi not punished for what he had done, he was also, of all things, appointed as prime minister, albeit for only four months. This was total misrule on the part of the emperor, and demonstrates the state of confusion into which imperial politics had fallen.

The third sub-period was the last four years, during which the preparations for war with Britain and the United States had been completed and there was open conflict. During this period as well, the prime ministerial baton was passed from Tojo to Koiso and then to Suzuki, but the appointment of these premiers was not characterized by any consistency. Koiso, moreover, had been involved with the abortive March Incident (an attempted coup of 1931). The establishing of a precedent whereby even someone who had been involved in a *coup d'état* could become prime minister was a very grave matter, suggesting that the emperor's appointment of a prime minister no longer held any authority.

If we compare in this way the leaders of each country during the war years, Germany, Italy and America can be said to have fought to the end with a commander-in-chief leading the country's forces into battle. Germany and Italy fought until their commander-in-chiefs were brought down. In the case of America, although Truman took control, his succession was forced upon the regime through an unforeseen occurrence. Britain, seeing the initial weakness of its leader, changed its leading player for the remainder of its war against Germany. By contrast Japan actually had 14 prime ministers chosen largely at random, and there was no plan behind the fighting of the war. Of the 14, those who were most responsible were, of course, Konoe and Tojo, but they themselves would probably have claimed that they had been unlucky, having been appointed when it already proved impossible to change the course of events.

Each of these prime ministers naturally bore little responsibility for Japan's defeat; that responsibility resided with the emperor, who presided over this incoherent state of affairs. In one British television programme looking back at the Second World War, Germany and Italy were represented by Hitler and Mussolini respectively, whereas Japan's supreme war leader was Hirohito. In Hirohito's case, however, not only was he unable to provide leadership during the war, he also failed completely in that he was totally unable even to choose appropriate men to be prime minister. During the First World War Max Weber criticized the German emperor, Wilhelm II, on the grounds that 'the emperor, as an amateur, should never meddle in politics or military affairs', but in Japan there was never any voice of warning such as Weber's. The emperor regarded the appointment of a suitable prime minister as one of his personal duties, and continued to carry out this selection to the best of his abilities, but looking back it is clear that these appointments possessed neither coherence nor philosophy; such appointments constituted a series of stopgap measures that left everything to chance.

In fact, the war should have been abandoned when Tojo resigned as prime minister. If this had happened the war in the Philippines, the deaths at Iwojima, the fighting in Okinawa, the bombing of the Japanese mainland, and the dropping of atomic bombs on Hiroshima and Nagasaki could all have been avoided. Of course unconditional surrender would have been hard to avoid even at this stage, so Japan would certainly have lost not only her territories in China, but Korea and Taiwan as well. Nevertheless, the deaths of over a million soldiers and ordinary civilians would have been averted, and there would have been hardly any war damage in Japan's cities. At the time, however, the emperor still believed that there was some slight possibility of victory, and so hoped that the enemy could be dealt a blow that would enable the war to be concluded on terms favourable to Japan. What a rosy assessment of the actual state of affairs!

By whom, then, was the desire for war with the United States and Britain articulated, and when was it formulated? It is clear that the final decision was taken by the emperor in the autumn of 1941, but it is also clear that neither the emperor nor Tojo, who was prime minister at the time, wished of their own accord to open hostilities. It would, moreover, be no exaggeration to say that most of the rest of Japan's leaders, the majority of the people, and even sensible members of the military had little spontaneous desire for war either. However, there did exist among the population one group of people, in whom social circumstances had instilled a set of beliefs that was fundamentally jingoistic.

What had shaped such a creed included, as mentioned above, the sense of grudge against the countries of the West stemming from events such as the unequal treaties of the late Tokugawa period, the Siberian Expedition at the end of the First World War, and the subsequent demand for withdrawal, and issues of racial discrimination. Some of these individuals provoked incidents in Manchuria, assassinated important individuals in acts of terrorism, and even claimed that their illegal activities were acts of patriotism undertaken for the emperor. Such acts should have been harshly punished by emperor and government early on, as a clear demonstration of the authorities' determination not to allow such acts to be condoned on the grounds of 'patriotic activity'.

However, this was also the time of the genesis of the left-wing movement, and the members of the ruling élite, concerned that a revolution of the kind that had taken place in Russia might occur in Japan as well, regarded the existence of patriots as a necessity for the protection of their own position. It was normal practice for patriotic criminals either to escape punishment altogether, or to receive only a light penalty. After the establishment of Manchukuo, many of them were expelled from the home islands (Japan), but were able to circulate freely in outlying territories (Manchukuo).

These so-called patriots also began to denounce freedom of thought. Many individuals, including Kawakami Hajime and other leftist thinkers, liberals such as Minobe Tatsukichi, Takigawa Yukitoki and Kawai Eijiro, as well as members of the liberal left such as Hani Goro, Miki Kiyoshi and Kuno Osamu, were imprisoned, or had their activities restricted. This suppression of thought was particularly severe during the second sub-period, from 1936 to 1941. It resulted in a total disappearance of moderate ideas, and apart from the patriotic ideologues, other thinkers effectively went into retirement. This state of affairs was extremely dangerous for the monarchic system as well, but because the emperor himself had become a pawn of the patriotic camp little could be done about it. It goes without saying that liberal thinkers and the peaceable majority of the population ceased to be able to express their opinions, let alone show open resistance.

The same could be said of the mass media – newspaper companies and publishers. They found it easy to disguise themselves to save their own skins, and became cheerleaders for those who had once been their enemies. The Japanese people demonstrated their lack of moral backbone and integrity by rushing forward to take on new guises as well. In the autumn of 1941, when national calls for 'punishment' for Britain and the United States reached a crescendo, it had already become impossible even for Tojo to subdue this frenzy. It has already been mentioned how it was Tojo's opinion that if at this point Japan had accepted American demands in order to avoid war, conflict would probably have erupted within Japan itself. In this Tojo's assessment of the situation was quite correct. At that stage, the only course that remained open to the emperor and Tojo if they were to preserve their own lives was an initiation of hostilities.[9]

Moreover, during the second sub-period Japan carried through its strategy of tying its fate to that of Germany. This was done through the German-Japanese Anti-Comintern Pact, and the Triple Alliance with Germany and Italy. On top of that it increasingly proved impossible in Japan for students and school pupils to avoid labour service, along the lines of the *Arbeitdienst* required of young people in Germany. In all sectors of Japanese society, in politics, in diplomacy, in military affairs, in the economy and in academia, the Anglo-American faction declined, and the pro-German faction was dominant. Japan had already become 'a Nazi state without a Hitler' or 'a Nazi state from below'.

At the same time the Emperor was elevated to the position of a god. Those individuals who sought to keep their distance from such fanatical nationalist ideas became social pariahs, and as a result had to be prepared even for imprisonment or death. Although the Emperor was a weak creature incapable of imposing his own wishes, he was himself a pacifist, and should not, therefore, be regarded as the Hitler of a Japanese Nazi state. I believe that it is a mistake and a distortion of the truth to view the Emperor as any kind of dictator. The Emperor was a man of weak character, who was not only unable to prevent war and but also collaborated with those who desired it.

It remains the case, however, that outside Japan, and particularly during the war, Hirohito was regarded as a Japanese Hitler, and it is perhaps inevitable that people should have reached such a view. The worst case scenario was that there was a strong possibility of the Emperor's being charged with war crimes over his war responsibility. Despite this America, as the leader of the allied camp, overruled the objections of the other allies in not bringing the Emperor to trial. As will be seen below, this decision was, from the American perspective, especially over the long term, a pretty drastic measure.

Recently people in Japan have been saying that the reason that the Emperor was not charged was that if he had been put on trial it would have caused immediate disturbances within the country. The Japanese, it is argued, would have fought to the death against the American forces when they attempted to suppress the unrest, and America's main aim was to avoid the human casualties that this would cause. My feeling is that this is at the most only one small part of the reason why the Emperor was not put on trial. This is because the impact of the question of the Emperor was far from being as dramatic as claimed by supporters of this theory, at least as far as the short-term effects are concerned. It is just not conceivable that, with the war ended, the Japanese people, relieved to be free from so many years of conflict in China and the Pacific, and suffering from conditions of acute food scarcity, should have fought to the death against the American army.

Even in the later stages of the war itself Japan had already lost its will to fight. For that reason it is likely that the Japanese army would have surrendered across the country to American troops landing on the Japanese mainland even without the dropping of the atomic bombs by the United States. There certainly existed an element within the population whose will to resist can be said to be fanatical, but it was to the end just one element. The country no longer possessed the capacity for organized resistance on land, at sea and in the air. The martial spirit had withered away, and military discipline was in total disarray.

Since the American forces stationed in Japan are likely to have been well aware of this situation, America, too, would probably have understood that major unrest would not have occurred in Japan even if the Emperor had been put on trial. Thus while the statement that the exemption of the Emperor from war crimes charges was 'in order to avoid futile fatalities among American troops' would have been easily accepted by most of the American people, people familiar with the situation in Japan at the time would have shaken their heads in disbelief at such a pretext. A far more persuasive reason was that 'the Emperor must not be punished in order to keep Japan in the Western camp in the coming Cold War'. Such a reason, however, could not be stated openly in the hearing of the Soviet Union. It is my belief, therefore, that America advanced this fraudulent reason in order to conceal its real motive.

It seems to me that this is a convincing conjecture. After the Tokyo war-criminals trial was closed in 1948, the Korean war started in 1950. If the Emperor had been put on trial, the American troops in Japan would have met, at the time of the Korean War, a huge anti-American movement involving the right-wing as well as the left-wing students and activists. It should be remembered that those Americans who helped the Emperor evade severe punishment were Herbert Hoover, former President of USA, General MacArthur, US Pacific Commander, Joseph Grew, US ambassador to Japan at the time of the outbreak of the War and Deputy Secretary of State at the time of Japan's surrender and General B. Fellers, MacArthur's aide and the counterpart of Terasaki. They were all fiercely anti-communist. Thus, on the American side the preparation for the cold war started in September, 1945 when MacArthur saw the Emperor for the first time.

VI

As a result of the defeat the position of the Emperor changed. Neither the people nor the Allies have inquired into the responsibilities of the Showa Emperor closely, but the Emperor soon ceased to act as the head of state. 'Symbol' was the special concept devised to describe the position of the emperor, and the Emperor is not seen as the head of state, i.e. the ruler, but, rather, the focus of national unity. Japan was changed into a country with a form of government unique in the world. Where an individual can be designated as the focus of national unity, that individual is normally a monarch or a constitutional monarch. It seems only proper that an individual who has not been given even the position of a constitutional monarch should not be able to serve as a focus of national unity. As a result of Japan's defeat the

Japanese emperor ceased to have any involvement in politics, except for very trivial affairs of state. Even so, he has come to be respected as the focus of national unity, and has continued to be treated cordially by the Japanese people. If this is the kind of national polity desired by the Japanese people (and I think that this is, in fact, the case), then the national polity can be said to have been preserved. However, in the sense that this situation is very different from the national polity that the members of the imperial conference at the end of the war sought to maintain, the national polity has also been transformed.

Not just in politics, but in relation to education as well, the position of the Emperor has changed considerably. Up until Japan's defeat the system was one in which the Emperor, through his rescripts, could intervene in the education of the people to encourage the development of the national spirit in a specific direction. In this sense Japan was a country where both education and politics were subject to imperial rescripts, just like China in the Qing period, or earlier.

Of these imperial pronouncements the most important included the Imperial Rescript on Education (*Kyoiku Chokugo*) and the Imperial Rescript to Soldiers and Sailors (*Gunjin Chokuyu*). There are even now in Japan many people who approve much of the content of the Imperial Rescript on Education. The historian Hayashi Kentaro (former president of Tokyo University), for example, has described the Rescript in the following words:

> The Rescript certainly did not mark an attempt to assert the divine status of the Emperor, and his position as the root of all virtue. Instead it presented universal moral precepts found in both past and present, and in both east and west, as the injunctions of the ancestors, which had to be adhered to by the Emperor along with his subjects. (*Bungei Shunju ni Miru Showa Shi* [Showa History seen through *Bungei Shunju*], vol.4 [Bunshun Bunko], pp. 456–7)

However, to think along these lines is a mistake. Hayashi says that the Emperor stated that these precepts should be observed because they were the injunctions of the ancestors, but the Rescript itself writes that they should be observed because they are 'the injunctions of our Imperial Ancestors'. Although for the Japanese to disregard their own individual ancestors and give special treatment to the ancestors of the Imperial family cannot be said quite to amount to deification of the emperor, it does tacitly imply that the Emperor is, in both human and ethical terms, superior to any other member of the population. Moreover Hayashi asks what was wrong when all the Emperor was attempting to do was to uphold 'universal moral precepts found in both east and west'. What was wrong with the Imperial Rescript on Education was not the core values that it claimed to support, such as filial piety towards one's parents and good relationships with one's friends. The problem lies in why the Emperor, the country and the Ministry of Education interfered in moral issues that should have been the concern of individual Japanese, issuing orders like 'the whole nation should be of one mind' and 'there must be but one virtue'. Morality cannot be sustained by edicts. As long as the emperor and the government tried to teach morality with this sort of attitude, the people of Japan could never understand the foundation of morality, which is that 'the spirit itself, or else the people themselves, should be completely free'.

The attempts of the Emperor and the government to control the thinking of the people, to brainwash them, in the name of the Emperor is, I think, the worst evil of the many evils attendant on the Emperor system, and it was imperial rescripts that were used by the Emperor system prior to the war as a tool for this purpose. It was done, moreover, in a very grand (and very extensive) stage setting. On national commemoration days students at all schools would gather in their respective assembly halls, to listen to their head teacher reading aloud the Imperial Rescript. The head teacher would wear formal Western dress and white gloves, and opening the Japanese style scroll on which the Rescript was written, would read it out slowly in an dignified voice. When the reading was finished the scroll would be calmly rolled up and returned to the box in which it was kept. The whole exercise would probably take at least 10 or 15 minutes, during which time the pupils had to remain standing, their heads bowed, listening to the Rescript.

It was a comic hybrid Western-Japanese ceremony. For the younger primary school pupils it had no meaning whatsoever. As students went up through the years of schooling the meaning of the Rescript became clearer, but even when they did understand, learning that the purpose of all morality, including brothers, sisters, husbands and wives getting on with each other, was to 'guard and maintain the prosperity of the Imperial Family coeval with heaven and earth', some older middle school and high school students began to dispute whether this was the real purpose of ethical principle. There were even some students who criticized the behaviour of the ancient emperors who had quarrelled with their siblings, sometimes killing each other. Once they got to high school, students such as these were far from being in the minority.

This kind of ceremony was not just to eradicate dissent, it was also utilized as a tool in the politics of fear. When I was a middle school student the son of General Ushiroku (also a young army officer) killed himself (through disembowelment) after making a mistake in reading the Imperial Rescript to Soldiers and Sailors. This was publicized as the story of a praiseworthy deed. One reason why the Japanese after the war hated the state so much was that up until the end of the conflict the system had been shockingly premodern or authoritarian. After the war any connection between religious beliefs and the state was severed, but because many of the Japanese people did not have strong religious convictions and did not regard the Emperor worship as the state religion, this move had little effect on Japanese people in general. We may still observe that both thought and education became more independent of the state than had been the case before the war, and Rescript-driven education was buried at least on the explicit surface, along with the 'Emperor system'.

It was not just the actions of the people that were controlled by the Imperial Rescript. It also stipulated the behaviour required of the Emperor. Right at the end of the rescript the Emperor stated the following:

> All the above things to be observed by the people have been laid down by the ancestors of the Imperial Family and successive Emperors as the conduct that must be followed by the people. For that reason I believe that the Emperor himself must also act in accordance with these precepts, possessing virtue in common with the people.

As these words show, it was not just the behaviour of the people that was being laid down by the Rescript, but the standards of behaviour of the Emperor as well.

In itself this was not a problem. However the rationale as to why the people had to behave in this way resides in the statement that the ancestors of the Imperial Family and successive Emperors had said that this had to be so. This meant that the Ise Shrine, dedicated to the Great Goddess Amaterasu, ancestor of the Emperor, was the source of Japanese morality, and it became the most important place in Japan for Japanese, and particularly for the emperor. The Ise Shrine is located near the sea in Ise Bay, around 240 kilometres from Tokyo as the crow flies.

Although for the military the defence of Tokyo was far more important than that of Ise Bay, for the Emperor the question of the defence of Ise Bay became an issue of major national importance. This was because the Ise Shrine and Atsuta Shrine on the coast of Ise Bay contain the three sacred treasures which mark the imperial line, and if they had been destroyed or fallen into the hands of the Americans the Emperor would have been left without proof of his legitimacy. At the end of the period of the internal war between the north and south dynasties of the Imperial Family (1338–92), the Southern Dynasty, which was the legitimate line, handed over the three sacred treasures to the Northern Dynasty, which thereafter produced one generation of emperor after another. Even Emperor Hirohito came from the Northern line, and there was an understanding that because he was the holder of the sacred treasures he should also hold the position of emperor. This kind of fetishism, whereby sacred treasures were valued more than bloodline, lay behind the Emperor's own perception of the national polity. While possession of the sacred treasures was mere evidence of legitimacy, they also had a substantive importance over and above being such evidence.

The imperial ancestor (the founder of the empire) was not a concrete, designated historical individual, but an imaginary figure from way back in Japan's past. Even so, obeying the will of the founder of the empire was more important for the emperor than anything else. In Japan the wishes of the 'imperial ancestor' were the fountainhead of justice and legitimacy. In that sense it was equivalent to the word 'heaven' in China. There was one difference, however. While under the rule of 'heaven' opportunities were open to everyone, 'imperial ancestor' was a highly discriminatory term. No one apart from the members of the imperial family, who were the descendants of the imperial ancestor, could ever aspire to the position of emperor. In China, by contrast, any dynasty that lost the mandate of 'heaven' ended up losing its power as well. A different dynasty compatible with the will of heaven would take up the position of ruler. Thus whereas in China it was possible for there to be revolution, in Japan there was created a 'national polity' that rendered any revolution impossible.

It was, of course, not always clear in China either what the will of 'heaven' actually was. The ruler was not chosen in accordance with the manifest will of heaven. The ruler obtained the position of emperor as the result of bloody struggles in the actual world, and the result of this selection process was regarded as showing the will of heaven. If this sort of will of heaven is treated as a 'revealed preference' theoretic, then the transcendent respect for the concept of 'heaven' ceases to exist. The will of the people in a democratic political system can also be construed as a 'revealed preference' theoretic. Thus any comparison of the Japanese idea of respect for the emperor, the Chinese belief in dynastic change and Western democratic thought must suggest that the first of these three stands in strong contrast to the other two, which have some similarity with each other.

At the time of Japan's defeat at the end of the Pacific War what Japan's ruling elite most feared, therefore, was revolution, and it was for that reason that 'preservation of the national polity' was absolutely essential. The kind of national polity that had emerged was a reflection of the contemporary circumstances at the time when the country of Nihon (Emperor Keitai) was established. As mentioned earlier, in Japan the Yamato Emperors were internally divided and in decline, or perhaps Emperor Keitai himself led a revolt. Whatever the case, the rulers believed that the most important thing was to ensure the continuation of the dynasty. The powerful Sui dynasty, which had taken control in China at the time of Emperor Sushun, the seventh emperor of Keitai's dynasty, fell to defeat at the hands of the Tang only 29 years later. Having experienced such events, the major object of concern of the imperial family at the time was how to prevent such a disaster from occurring to them. They were also aware of the destruction of Paekche and Wa. Their most important priority was that they should rule Japan 'coeval with heaven and earth'. Along with asserting their unlimited rule over Japan into the future, the dating back of their rule into the distant past also had to be stated as fact. This led to earlier history being modified and expanded upon to produce a story favourable to them.

A further measure to forestall revolution was to determine the status of all families outside the imperial line, and to determine the structure of government in such a way as to preclude any change in this ranking.

We noted above how in 587 China introduced an examination system, adopting an extremely progressive method of making appointments by choosing bureaucrats in accordance with their results in the examinations. In Japan, however, ranking at court came to be determined according to family status, and those whose family status was low could never hope for high position. In fact if we look at politics in Japan during the sixth to eighth centuries, it is apparent that the main political concern was how to bring the blood line of one's own family together with the blood line of the imperial family. Imperial princes were classified according to the family from which their mother came, and there was political strife within the imperial family marked by the killing of imperial princes born of different mothers. Whereas China was extremely progressive, Japan created an extremely conservative state structure. This demonstrates the extent to which Japan was a country that went in morbid fear of revolution. Japan, which lived in the shadow of China's influence, and learnt from it, yet created a country that was in strong contrast to that of China.

In older times the tension that existed between China and Japan was rooted in the mutual antagonism between what Marxists would term the superstructure of the two countries (their 'national polities', the ethos of the people, their customs, etc.). This was certainly not because their substructures (economic structures) differed greatly from each other. As we shall see in Lecture 2, even in the postwar years, when China became a communist country, and Japan reverted from being a planned economy to becoming a democratic one, it is possible to regard both their economies as belonging to the same category, namely that of 'capitalism from above'. Even in an avowedly socialist economy there becomes apparent at some stage the trends found in capitalism from above, and even Japan, regarded as a mature capitalist economy, has continued to be guided by the state as it was before.

There are many, however, who would oppose this view. First of all, Japan was overwhelmingly influenced by Chinese culture. To be quite blunt, Japan is a country that copied both China and Korea. We have already seen, however, how in order to create a national polity in which revolution could never occur the Japanese equated 'heaven' with the current ruling dynasty, and devised the idea of conflating 'heaven' and god. Thus the rule of the emperor was close to a theory of divine right arguing that imperial status was granted by the gods, but it was more powerful than a simple theory of divine right. This was because the national philosophy of Japan acknowledged that the emperor who ruled the country of Japan was himself a god, and that this emperor (god) could therefore not bestow the status of emperor on anyone apart from himself. Moreover, there could be no criticism of the emperor precisely because he was emperor, i.e. 'heaven'. The Chinese emperor would pray to heaven, but the Japanese emperor did not pray to heaven. If he did pray, or ask for help, it was only to his own ancestors, i.e. his imperial ancestors, and in that sense the Japanese imperial family was self-contained. This meant that the Japanese people did not permit revolution, and, therefore, were arrogant.

Since a god rules over all places, such a god-emperor would also be the ruler of all territories. During the period when Japan was secluded from outside contacts the concept of 'all the corners of the world under one roof' (*hakko ichiu*) was not a dangerous one. However, as Japan was opened up to such contacts this concept of the emperor became inseparable from imperialist thoughts of annexing other parts of the world. What had led to Japanese believing in such dangerous ideas was that at the time of the founding of the country Northeast Asia had been dominated by the vast Chinese Empire, and this was an extremely dangerous environment for a small country such as Japan. As early as the eighth century, therefore, a fierce nationalism burned in the hearts of the Japanese people, and in particular in the hearts of the ruling classes.

This fierce nationalism led the Japanese to reinterpret the culture that had reached them from China, and to change it into something different. For example, Japan, like China, is a Confucian country, but Japanese Confucianism is not the same as Chinese Confucianism. The virtues deemed important by Confucianism include benevolence, righteousness, knowledge, trust, loyalty and filial piety, but although the Japanese are well aware that Confucius regarded benevolence (*jin*) as the cardinal virtue, hardly anything has been taught in Japan about the virtue of benevolence. In Japan loyalty (*chu*) has been conceived as the most important virtue, and regarded as taking priority over all other virtues. The ranking of the virtues in Japan has therefore been different from that in China. The interpretation of the virtues has also differed between the two countries. In China loyalty (*chu*) refers to fidelity to one's own conscience, but in Japan it means serving one's lord with fidelity. After the modern unification of the country the lord to whom loyalty was due was no longer a feudal ruler, but the emperor, so loyalty meant giving up one's life for the emperor in order to prove one's loyalty to him. For that reason it is quite possible for a person who is disloyal in the Chinese sense of the word still to be loyal according to the Japanese interpretation.

Japanese Confucianism is thus not the same as Chinese Confucianism. Both versions have in common the Confucian classics, but their interpretations of them have been very different. The relationship between the two therefore resembles that between Catholicism and Protestantism, which largely rely on the same Bible. Max Weber made clear how these two religious denominations, resembling each other but at the same time different, led to the appearance of very major differences in people's daily lives and activities. In just the same way, in Asia Japanese Confucianism and Chinese Confucianism led to significant differences in the behaviour of the two peoples. In my earlier book, *Why Has Japan 'Succeeded'?* (1982), I emphasized this as the knife-edge property whereby a difference in ethos influences the outcome of people's earthly existence. I used this knife-edge property to explain the paradox whereby China, a country with a far more advanced culture than Japan, was overtaken by Japan in the modernization stakes. Chinese Confucianism has emphasized literature, Japanese Confucianism the military arts. The literary arts meant respect for knowledge of the classics, or the ability to write poetry. A military emphasis brought with it the promotion of science. It is not surprising that China should have lagged behind Japan in building modern capitalist industry. That Confucianism was also the product of the eighth century sense of crisis discussed above. It was only this kind of Confucianism that could successfully coexist with the fundamental concept of the national polity, i.e. the concept of Japan's being ruled over by an eternally unbroken line of emperors coeval with heaven and earth.

Secondly, both China and Japan have long been bureaucratic countries, but whereas China selected bureaucrats through the examination system, Japan stuck with a system of family pedigree, even under the progressive Prince Shotoku. Examinations for bureaucratic appointments had already started in China several years before Shotoku became regent, but although the examinations were probably a pretty hot topic in China Shotoku did not seek to introduce them to Japan. How far an individual could rise at the Japanese court was determined not by a person's ability, but according to the rank of the family into which he had been born. The most important official posts were therefore monopolized by a few leading families. It was not just the court that operated in this way. A similar structure was adopted by the Tokugawa *Bakufu*. They only began to take men of talent into government service after they had at last realized that their national crisis would not be overcome if they continued to stick to the traditional way of governance. These two points suggest that while Japan in many respects resembles China the countries are polar opposites in others. However, in the following respect, emphasized by G.W.F. Hegel as a Chinese characteristic, Japan is very 'Chinese', or, as we shall see later, even more 'Chinese' than the Chinese. To use Hegel's words[10]:

In China there still exists no element of what we might call autonomy. There is no resistance to the communal influence that consumes the individual will, or no awareness on the part of any individual of his own will. ... The collective will directly dictates what the individual must do, and the individual follows dutifully, without reflection and without awareness. ... The main constituent upon which the collectivity directly rests is the emperor and the collectivity is then formed.

The greatest respect has to be paid to the emperor. ... In China the ideal ruler and the ideal education for a ruler are splendidly realised, and the righteousness, happiness and security of the country as a whole is bound up with the capability of the individual at the apex of a ranking system that continues unbroken.

It is clear from the above that the emperor is the heart of the country, and that everything revolves around him and comes back to him, and how the happiness of the land and the people are bound up with him. ... The emperor is the supreme holder of authority. Only he holds a position near to heaven, while other individuals are far removed from it. ... The emperor always addresses his people with dignity, with the good intentions and sympathy of a father, but the people have no feelings that he is proud, believing only that he was born only to carry on the burden of imperial authority, with all its majesty.

If in the above extracts the Chinese word for emperor was changed to the word used to refer to the Japanese emperor (Tenno), his words would be applicable not only to China and Japan when he was giving his lectures at the start of the nineteenth century but also to Japan right up until the end of the Pacific War. Moreover, in the Japanese case, not only was there no heaven above the emperor, the emperor was himself equivalent to heaven, so the emperor was supreme, matchless and absolute. This was the meaning of the 'Emperor system', the national polity of Japan up until the time of defeat.

The Emperor system was not merely a system of monarchy. Under the Emperor system the people had no knowledge of what freedom was. They all followed the wishes of the emperor, regardless of the rights and wrongs of the case. It is true that after the Meiji Restoration Japan introduced modern technology, and gave the appearance on the surface of being a modern state, but her spirit remained totally premodern. As long as the war was only a war between Japan and China the issue of the national polity was not that important, but the Pacific War was fought against countries whose national systems were entirely different. To use Hegel's terms, in America and Britain people as a whole were conscious of their freedoms as people, while Japan was a country in which 'only one person (the Emperor) knows that he is free', and everyone else acted in accordance with the dictates of that one person. The war is often said to have been a war between east and west, but it can more correctly be termed a war between the premodern and the modern. What is shocking about this, is that the war was started by the premodern against the modern, but not *vice versa*.

Lecture 2
Vicissitudes of Nations:
A Materialist View

I

We at last have to think about what a nation is. There exist two kinds of groups in society: associations governed by 'formal' relations which have been artificially created by the will of the people, and where rights and obligations are clearly laid down; and those in which people are brought together in 'informal' relations, whether or not constituted by man or nature. The former is referred to as a man-made association or a society of interest, the latter as a community, but they are often referred to by the German terms *Gesellschaft* for the former, and *Gemeinschaft* for the latter. A company or a school is clearly a group based on interest, while families, races and religious groups are communities. State schools, unlike private schools, are not in search of profit, but are nevertheless societies of interest acting according to certain clearly stated rules.

Communities such as families and peoples are not as a rule chosen according to the wishes of the people concerned, but in the case of marriage it is clearly possible to choose one's family community. Communities based on things such as language or customs cannot, for the most part, be chosen. In the case of a community of belief, however, the choice rests with the wishes of the individual concerned. On the other hand there are some cases in which the character of schools is hardly different from that of communities of belief, and they can be properly thought of as school communities. This is particularly true where there is a keen enthusiasm when a school is first being established. This would seem to have been the case with the Nankai

University in its early years. This shows that an interest society and a community are not clearly separated, but are in some cases linked to each other, the border between them blurred. (Students from other countries at LSE say to their teachers that when they have come back to London and visited the School as graduates, they have had the feeling of coming back home. I, too, have had this said to me on several occasions.)

In the context of all these different kinds of society a state possesses a very particular character. It is on the one hand a *Gemeinschaft* whose members share a collective destiny, but it also has a man-made governing organization (government), making it a *Gesellschaft*. A state that does not possess such a framework (thus meaning that it is not a *Gesellschaft*) can continue to be a nation (or a people), but it cannot be a state in the proper sense of the term. For that reason a state is a kind of hybrid society that must at the same time be both *Gesellschaft* and *Gemeinschaft*. A state of this kind is therefore referred to in English as a nation-state. In as far as a nation state is a hybrid society of this kind, it cannot coexist with unadulterated egoism. As long as they are a people, every individual must render service to the nation-state. Such service, however, has to be interpreted extremely broadly. The government and the armed forces should not devise their own rigid concept of service to the state; they should not, in any case, demand of the people this service in a rigorously specified form. At least some room for choice must be available to the people. On the other side, the people have to respond by willing to undertake some service or other though it may be a service which is not very preferable from the viewpoint of the government. It is a mistake to bring up people to be unwilling to undertake any service whatsoever, and in Japan, especially given the absence of compulsory military service after the war, the Japanese have been brought up in ignorance of how they might make a contribution to the community.

This is the fault of Japan's postwar constitution and the postwar education system. People cannot detach themselves from their community and live only in society of interest, so they have somehow to be taught the manners and morality required to live in a community. However, since nationalism in its worst form ran riot during the war years, people regarded the morality of the community as a bad thing. However, while excessive nationalism is bad, no nationalism, or too little of it, is certainly not a good thing either.

What kind of nationalism would therefore be appropriate? Clearly nationalism must not be in conflict with universalism. Nationalism is essentially the egoism of the nation-state, and universalism a denial of such egoism. It is therefore hard for the two to coexist. Nevertheless, people waver between being egoistic and rejecting egoism, and so as far as nations are concerned as well, people's ideas may be expected to waver between egoism at one end of the spectrum, and universalism at the other. Thus at any particular time it is possible for an appropriate balance to be maintained between the two. This was the case with Japan, too, in the past.

Let us take a concrete historical example. In 1864, four years before the Meiji Restoration, the four powers of America, Britain, France and Holland bombarded Shimonoseki in Choshu domain. At that time Japan was geographically divided among numerous domains (*han*), and the people within each domain were divided according to social status between the four classes of warrior, farmer, artisan and merchant. The people of Chikuzen on the opposite shore to Choshu therefore regarded the conflict purely as one between Choshu domain and the four powers, and watched the battle from the beach as if they were watching a sports contest. Similarly the population of Choshu apart from the warrior caste thought of it as a battle between the four powers and the Choshu *samurai*, putting themselves in the position purely of onlookers. Their conduct was thus strongly universalistic. They assisted the wounded Choshu warriors, and at the same time helped soldiers from the other side. This was not a phenomenon specific purely to Choshu. A more or less similar situation would probably have occurred if any of the Japanese domains had been attacked by foreign troops. A nation-state had at this time yet to be established in Japan, and an awareness of nation was still weak.

At the time of the Manchurian Incident, however, the situation had changed completely. Although the incident was started illegally by a handful of soldiers from the Japanese army, the army failed to put them before a court martial. This was because they were soldiers of Japan. Universalism had already retreated to a level where national awareness was so exalted that it was subject neither to the law nor to the provisions of the army's criminal code. After that universalism retreated even further, and although the Pacific War was started by Japan's élite under pressure from the armed forces, nationalism in

Japan was so strong that the people as a whole were willing to fight under the slogan of 'total war'.

So is there some point in time between 1864 and 1931 where there was a proper balance between nationalism and universalism? My own view is that the time of the Russo-Japanese War marked a point of equilibrium between the two. General Nogi's treatment of General Stessel and his men after the surrender of Port Arthur, for example, was extremely courteous.

A further example is the action taken by Admiral Kamimura, commander-in-chief of the second squadron. The second squadron had been lying in wait in the Straits of Korea for the Russian squadron from Vladivostok, which was often seen in these waters. They eventually caught up with the Russian ships on 14 August 1904, and the squadron destroyed them in the sea off Ulsan Bay. The main strength of the Russian squadron was provided by the three ships *Ryurikku, Roshia* and *Guromoboi.* Kamimura first had the *Naniwa* and *Takachiho* attack the *Ryurikku* (a cruiser), and then himself led the *Izumo, Iwate, Azuma* and *Tokiwa* in pursuit of the other two. Running short of ammunition, though, they gave up the pursuit, and turned back to try and join in the sinking of the *Ryurikku.* (There is some debate as to whether or not this was a correct judgment to make.) However by this time the *Ryurikku* had already been sunk, and the *Naniwa* and *Takachiho* were rescuing the Russian sailors. Kamimura thereupon ordered the ships that he had been leading to rescue the enemy as well. Eventually the second squadron led by Kamimura, the fourth squadron and the ninth flotilla joined forces to rescue the enemy sailors.[1]

There can be a different view as to whether or not Kamimura's conduct was correct. He was fiercely criticized by nationalist individuals. Within the naval general staff, however, his action seems to have met with approval. A song in praise of Kamimura was sung by the navy as a war song even during the Pacific War, and volume 2 of the *History of the War at Sea 1904–5* compiled by the naval general staff contains a picture of the warship *Izumo* with the caption 'Japanese sailors chatting with Russian sailors brought on board the Izumo after the battle and provided with clothing'. For those confident that they had fought with a sense of fair play, the naval battle off Ulsan was certainly a good war.

Whatever the country, nationalism may not be said to be the supreme ethic in any absolute sense. It is, inevitably, only one partial ethic within a larger sense of being a group. This recognition is not, however, a new one. It was a problem directly addressed, and solved, by the loyalist *samurai* of the late Tokugawa period. The supreme ethical maxim for *samurai* at that time was loyalty to one's lord, which meant the lord of the domain to which a warrior belonged. Such feelings of loyalty were combined in the following way with a great loyalty towards the Emperor, which these loyalists had already begun to regard as being very important. Each domain lord owed loyalty to the *shogun* as head of the *Bakufu* (military government). The *shogun* in turn owed loyalty to the Emperor. Under such conditions there was no contradiction between the loyalty a samurai owed to his domain lord, and his loyalty to the Emperor.

Should the *shogun* act in a way contrary to the wishes of the Emperor, however, loyalty to the domain lord ceased to be loyalty to the Emperor. The loyalists were greatly concerned over this, and argued that under these circumstances the domain lord should discard his loyalty to the *shogun* and give his allegiance directly to the Emperor. Exactly the same problem confronted the Japanese people before and during the Second World War. That is to say, the Japanese state is just one element in a broader society, and as long as the actions of the state are compatible with the universal ethical values held by the peoples of the world, loyalty to the state can be regarded as ethically correct. However, when Japan's actions started to conflict with international morality, and they were faced with the question of the morality of the Japanese state on the one hand, and international morality on the other, people had to think carefully about choosing between the two. At the time, though, Japanese philosophers such as Nishida Kitaro and Watsuji Tetsuro did not give serious thought to this question. To that extent Japan must be said to be lacking in any consideration of universal morality.

We cannot know what they really thought, but superficially at least both Nishida and Watsuji made a pretence of 'giving up their lives for the Emperor'. As intellectuals, of course, they were unlikely to have been under any illusion that the Emperor was a god, and so what they did was hardly the result of any religious conversion to a belief in the divinity of the Emperor. In fact, the pressure that they would have come under had they not made any such pretence would have been horrific. On the other hand, the Emperor himself too had been subject to the authority of the Imperial Ancestors. The will of the Emperor was always presented to the Japanese people as having been approved by the 'divine spirits of the Imperial Ancestors', and not a single voice could be raised in opposition to anything approved by these imperial ancestors. In that sense, as I have already said on more than one occasion, prior to the country's defeat the Japanese people had no concept of any broader society or world of ideas beyond their own nation of Japan. They all, including Nishida and Watsuji, were just like the inhabitants of a medieval absolutist state.

II

What are the units, then, that transcend the nation? It is probably fair to say that it used to be only the world (*die Welt*) that did this. By *die Welt* we also mean the people in the world, that is those in the indefinitely large circle of acquaintance, so that it is a hard place to be. A sufficiently warm relationship according to which family and fellow countrymen coexist interdependently can be expected only as something quite exceptional, or a matter of chance. All one finds is furious competition taking place between them. Not just economic theory, but the theory of the interest society (*Gesellschaft*) focuses on competition, and as far as national economies are concerned analysis tends only to extend to the man-made aspects in national life. On the other hand we have the community aspects of national life, and in order to analyse these aspects we have had to devise a sociology relating to parents and children, husbands and wives, brothers and sisters, neighbours, analysing communities such as households, villages and cities.

However, if we accept that *die Welt* is indeed the only thing that transcends the nation, analysis of its economic aspects goes no further than analysis of world markets, which are associations that are purely man-made. Moreover, even if the sociological aspects are analysed, the concepts utilized in analysis of the community are of very little use. War and other international relations are explained purely in terms of egoism, on the assumption that each nation selects the means commensurate with achieving its objectives, and acts accordingly. This was the idea at least until the end of the Second World War.

After the war, however, the world rapidly ceased to be a place where unrelated persons live together. Like the nation, the world came to possess simultaneously the character of both *Gesellschaft* and

Gemeinschaft. There also existed in between nation and world federations of nations, larger than a nation, but smaller than the world as a whole. At present only the European Union (EU) has passed beyond infancy to enter into childhood, but if we think of the USA not so much as a nation state but rather as a federation of states, then the USA is well embarked on its youth. As we shall see later, it is possible that such a federation could be formed in Asia as well. It is apparent from the history of the EU that federations of this kind start off as economic communities – associations formed purely in the pursuit of gain. For them to function adequately, however, involves other social functions, and this results in their developing into an all-embracing union. If membership of the federation continues over some years or some tens of years, the peoples of the member countries before long form with each other relationships of friendship, sympathy and mutual understanding that transcend the nation state, and a federation *Gemeinschaft* is formed, just as in the past city communities have been built on the basis of the same kind of spiritual element.

My belief is that the postwar world is equipped with the material and technological conditions that make possible this kind of thing. The size of any community depends on the technologies available to it, including means of travel and transport, and the transmission of ideas. These technologies have developed remarkably since the war, so the scale of state formation that took place in the nineteenth and early twentieth centuries (i.e. the size of the nation states) was too small given the new technologies. The formation of the EEC after the war was not something that took place out of the blue, but even had a certain historical inevitability about it.

In fact the EEC, and particularly the European Coal and Steel Community out of which it developed, was something that had been explicitly called for by Keynes after the First World War.[2] This did not come into being at the time, however. Instead we had the appearance of men like Hitler, Mussolini and Tojo, each having been intent on aggrandizing his own nation. Their actions were no different from the imperialist behaviour of the nineteenth and early twentieth centuries, and in as far as they believed that the technologies of the time were compatible with the broader communities transcending the nation state that they envisioned, their misguided attempts, too, can probably be evaluated as 'mistaken works' in the long sweep of history. Whatever the case, technology today has developed to such an extent that the nation states of the nineteenth century model are too small, and will in due course over the next century have to become part of larger federations.

Federations of this kind are likely to develop as *Gemeinschaften* just as the nation states of the nineteenth century did. In the case of the Japanese, for example, at the end of the Tokugawa period awareness of Japan's being a single national entity was extremely low, but 40 years later it had developed to a level at which the country was sufficiently united to be able to fight against Russia, one of the world's great powers. The formation of a national consciousness accelerated, and only 30 years after that Japan had become a country of nationalism to the point of brutality.

The Meiji Restoration was essentially an attempt to bring together the various feudal domains of the Tokugawa period. A similar attempt was made in Italy, with unification achieved in 1861. The unification of Germany was achieved in 1871, but Friedrich List had articulated his theory of unification prior to that. Just as in the case of the European community the weapon was a common market, so List had asserted that the formation of a customs union was a prerequisite for the unification of Germany. Europe thus developed an array of strong nation states, and for a period these nation-states continued to fight with each other. Keynes' proposal for achieving peace mentioned earlier was virtually ignored.

A country unified along Listian lines needs to have nearby territories that can supply food and raw materials in order to ensure its own survival, and this idea was the precursor of Hitler's concept of *Lebensraum* (life space). Similarly the Japanese idea of the Greater East Asia Co-Prosperity Sphere had regard only to Japan's *Lebensraum*. It was based on a total absence of universalism and took no account of the *Lebensraum* of other countries. Nevertheless, it is possible to construct such a broader economic entity in such a way that (i) it becomes the *Lebensraum* for all the countries that belong to it, and (ii) it does not bring about a deterioration in the living conditions of those countries that remain outside it. I believe that the EU will develop into this sort of community, and that it is possible that similar federations will appear in other regions of the world.

Moreover, the world itself is no longer a place purely for the pursuit of interest, and is in the process of becoming a community. For one thing, the world is no longer unlimited in size. There is certainly going to be no change in the geographical size of the earth, but as far as the consumption of energy for its economic activities is concerned, the world is obviously year by year becoming smaller. The world is no longer a society devoid of shame in which anything goes. Nuclear incidents are a typical example of how the influence of key technologies will invariably affect several countries. Moreover unless both countries and individuals prove capable of self-discipline, global warming will be inevitable, to the extent that before long the earth will cease to be able to sustain life and will eventually burn up. The earth is reaching the point at which its inhabitants have to work together to protect it. This means that in the future it is likely to be impossible for federations of states to act as imperialists.

One of the 'theories' of sociology states that 'the community character of society is gradually becoming weaker, and the power of the interest society is over time becoming stronger'. From the perspective of this theory the world (as a pure *Gesellschaft*) is regarded as becoming an ever harder place to live in, and one where each person has to look to him or herself. In this view the cultures (*Kultur*) nurtured by the individual nation states will each lose their specific characteristics, until we are left with a world only of civilization (*Zivilisation*). This is because the former type of world is the product of a community society, the latter the product of man-made associations.

This kind of 'theory', however, is a line of thought supported by the *Zeitgeist* of the late nineteenth century, and one with which I cannot go along. One reason is that I do not believe in this theory of unilateral strengthening of man-made associations and weakening of communities. On the contrary, I consider that the strengthened man-made associations go on to create new communities. Since the newly formed communities differ from those of the past, their character is also likely to be different from that of their predecessors. There is, however, nothing new about this. Even within our own families there is a significant degree of difference between the relationship that we have with our parents, and that which we have with our children. That means that the character and culture of a federation of states will probably be quite different from those found in nation-states individually.

Moreover, the world itself is bound to develop communitarian aspects. Activities that increases global warming will have to be harshly punished. All countries are likely to have to recognise the authority of the international courts which make rulings on this sort of problem. The United Nations may well cease to be organized on the basis of membership of individual states, and be reconstituted as a federation of bodies such as the EU and the AU (Asian Union). The international courts judging problems such as nuclear testing or experiment would come to acquire greater powers. Once this stage was reached the idealistic Kellogg–Briand Pact and the new Japanese constitution could no longer be dismissed with a smile as the stuff of dreams. Moreover one important thing is that moves in this direction are an everyday occurrence, and events that are part of this process – for example, the meetings of G7 leaders – are being held according to a planned schedule. In 50 years time the situation in the world will be very different, and the UN will probably be starting to lay the foundations for a world government.

It must be stressed that this kind of trend does not rest on any kind of ideological idealism. What lies behind it, as I shall explain below, is the development of transport and communication technologies. Even today Concorde can take us round the world in 31 hours, probably less than the time required immediately after Japan's defeat for the people of southern Kyushu to travel to Tokyo. The world has thus shrunk to a point where it is smaller than was Japan 50 years ago. Technological developments will make the world ever smaller, and those technological foundations will bring about major changes in the superstructure built upon them. In the future risking one's life for Japan will probably be regarded like risking one's life for the selfish interests of Nagano Prefecture would be today. People have naturally come to act with regard to the interest of other prefectures as well.

However, when this happens people will start to be aware of a new and larger community transcending the nation, and it will no longer be possible for us to live if we turn our backs on such a community. When that time comes an education that prizes selfishness (for example, that of postwar Japan) will become a source of problems. The size and character of a community will change either gradually or rapidly in accordance with the development of technology, but in any period people have to contribute to the preservation and development of the larger community that is bound to exist.

It has been argued that sports requiring team play are extremely effective in instilling that kind of spirit into children, and that boy scout type activities are also important for the education of young people. In British schools students have to choose whatever they like out of this sort of practical activity and pursue that activity as one of their subjects. My own child chose to pilot an aeroplane, and after one term of training, flying solo in front of an instructor, which was pretty horrific, gave it up to work as a nurse in an old people's home. My generation was made to carry out military drill from the time we were at middle school, and if military training could be provided as an intellectual subject, I think that it could be an enjoyable subject. If students were permitted to discuss such things as the pros and cons of war at such and such a time, and the victory or defeat that would result, military drill could be of value in protecting the country in the true sense. Shouting at people in loud voices to advance was certainly not good training for protecting the country.

Whatever the case, we need to revise our school education so as to enhance the spirit of working for the group, by clarifying people's obligations to the community and applying the brake to an education that teaches nothing but selfishness.

III

What, then, are the circumstances that determine the size of a society, and in particular the size of a state? As I said earlier, while a state is a form of *Gemeinschaft* (community), it is at the same time a *Gesellschaft* (a man-made association). If we think a little more about each of these two kinds of association, with a view to making clear how the two are combined in the state, we may get some idea as to the emergence, development and disappearance of states.

In German the word *Gemeinschaft* has the meaning of the English word 'common'. The European Common Market is referred to in German as *Gemeinsamer Markt*. When people are tied together in a longlasting relationship, they start to share aspects of their lives. Many of those relationships are those resulting from birth, where there is no element of choice, such as between parent and child or brother and sister, but enduring relationships also include some for which people opt of their own free will, for example between husband and wife, or between neighbours.

The shared aspects of life resulting from enduring relationships include the need for collective ownership and collective defence. Living like this people engage in 'close relationships imbued with trust', relationships which before long develop into an exclusive intimacy. A feeling of unity is formed among people who are tied together by this kind of relationship. A society that nurtures such a feeling of unity is a *Gemeinschaft*. A family is a *Gemeinschaft* of the family line; village or hamlet *Gemeinschaften* are formed on the basis of the common ownership of fields, woods and pastures, while prior to the advent of modern capitalism cities were defence *Gemeinschaften*.

As opposed to this, *Gesellschaft* refers to a group of associates. By associates I mean other people chosen on purpose. It is not a relationship pledged for eternity, and can be dissolved. A *Gesellschaft* is a man-made association formed with the specific purpose of achieving some goal or other, an association which is disbanded once the objective has been achieved.

Even in the case of a society of this kind, however, should it take a long time for the objective to be achieved, and the society has to continue working to achieve it over a lengthy period, then the *Gesellschaft* can endure far longer than the life of just one individual. Under these circumstances its members are likely to retain their connection with it throughout their lives. Where this happens the members will be brought together in 'close relationships imbued with trust', and they will end up sharing an exclusive intimacy. This means that a *Gesellschaft* can produce a *Gemeinschaft*. The so-called Japanese-type company, for example, is one such *Gemeinschaft*.

What then are the reasons why the state as a *Gesellschaft* should expand or shrink? Let us start with some general ideas that are not limited just to the state. Take, for example, the phrases 'out of sight, out of mind' and 'strangers begin with brothers'. Even in the case of family communities based on blood ties, if a member's work leads him to move far away, the relationship naturally weakens, and eventually there is little awareness of being relatives. At the stage where means of transport are undeveloped, a family will operate an extended family system as long as its members all reside in the same village locality. However, if means of transport develop and some members end up living a long way away, it becomes very difficult to sustain the extended family system. Moreover, when man-made associations are at an undeveloped stage, there is relatively little division of labour, and parents and children, brothers and sisters, are all likely to do more or less the same sort of work. However, once there is a substantial division of labour within a society the chance is that parents will end up doing different work from each of their children. The result of this is that feelings of intimacy within the family based on members' undertaking the same kind of work become weaker. For that reason the scale of the family diminishes, at least as far as the extent of its feelings of intimacy is concerned. This reaches its limit in the contemporary nuclear family.

Over the course of time the size of the family thus shrinks, and the same phenomenon can be confirmed if the state is the unit of analysis. A typical example of this is the British Empire and the British Commonwealth. The British Empire comprised both sparsely inhabited regions to which the British emigrated in large numbers, creating British-type societies, and also extremely densely populated territories whose peoples were ruled by Britain. In the case of the first, the principle of 'out of sight, out of mind' applied. The colonies came to demand that they be permitted to make up their own minds on the question of independence from the mother country, and where that demand was not met, declared their intention of securing their autonomy, even at the cost of war, as happened in the American case. By this means they acquired the status of self-governing territories, and then after the First World War the status of independent countries as a result of their contributions during the conflict. They ceased to be part of the British Empire, and instead formed with Britain a 'common-wealth'. The period after the First World War was thus one of a dual system of both empire and commonwealth, but even before the Second World War one of the territories controlled by Britain (not a colony) was aspiring in the future to leave the empire and join the commonwealth instead. This was India. Britain itself argued that it would grant India the right of autonomy in the future, but when that time came India should remain within the Empire. However, in recognition of India's achievements during the Second World War, when the country incurred some 200,000 war dead on Britain's behalf, Britain subsequently acquiesced in India's leaving the Empire and becoming part of the commonwealth.

There are many Japanese who believe that the collapse of the British Empire and that liberation of India, Burma and the other British-ruled territories in Asia came as a result of the Pacific War, and that herein lies the significance of the war for world history. The historical facts indicated above, however, show that such an understanding is mistaken, at least as far as Britain is concerned. If there was a war that brought about the collapse of the British Empire, it was the First

World War, and by the time of the Second World War the major elements in the empire had already seceded from it. The most that it did, therefore, was to give a stimulus to the building of the Commonwealth. What provided the stimulus, moreover, was not any antipathy towards empire or the outcome of any rebellion, but the result of contributions to the empire. This is in line with the improvement in status of American Japanese as the result of their contribution during the war.

My belief is that what determines the size of a state is the level of technology, including the level of development of weaponry, transport and means of communication, but this does not necessarily mean that the two develop in a balanced manner. In the case of Japan there was virtually no change in either weaponry or means of transport from the Nara period (710–784) through to the Ashikaga period (1338–1573). Using these same technologies a unified country was formed in Japan comprising the territories of Honshu, Shikoku and Kyushu, but this was too big a country given the means of transport available at the time. In line with the rule 'out of sight, out of mind', the Minamoto clan, who were descended from the Imperial family, seized political autonomy, setting up their own independent fiefdom. The same phenomenon appeared prior to Minamoto's Kamakura *Bakufu* although in a less obvious form, resulting in a situation in which the central government had no choice but to acknowledge the privileges of the *shoen* (manors). Before too long Japan also proved too large for a *Bakufu* that depended on military force, and in the closing years of the Muromachi *Bakufu*, the *Bakufu* ceased to be able to rule the whole country. Japan entered a period of civil war during which the country broke up into a number of separate 'countries' which fought against each other.

At this time weapons in Japan experienced a revolutionary development. This was because muskets and cannons were imported from Europe. The civil war was brought to an end and Japan unified through the force of these new weapons. As far as means of land transport were concerned, however, there was no such epoch-making transformation. The Tokugawa *Bakufu* therefore relinquished the idea of establishing a central government that would rule directly over the whole country, and instead created a system of indirect rule, dividing the country into a large number of separate territories, the government of each entrusted to a government from one of the clans. This proved to be an extremely clever device, and one that continued until the Meiji period, when the balance between weaponry and means of transport was reversed.

Under a feudal system, if the territory obtained through force is too large, the ruler grants the land to his subordinates in return for military service whenever he should need it. This was the kind of master–follower relationship that existed between the Shogun as head of the *Bakufu* and the various domain lords in the Tokugawa period. The *Bakufu*-domain system was therefore one which would rapidly have collapsed, had the development of technology reduced the size of Japan to the scale where the country could be unified. By the closing years of the Tokugawa period, when intercourse with Western nations became a matter of frequency, and people came to be familiar with the technologies developed in the West, both *Bakufu* and domains were convinced that their structure of rule had become out of date.

That this recognition was shared both by the *Bakufu* and by those domains which opposed the *Bakufu* was a basic reason for the peaceful surrender of Edo castle. Knowledge of new technologies (even though they had yet successfully to acquire them) rendered the *Bakufu*-domain system and the Tokugawa superstructure obsolete, resulting in the formation for the first time in Japan of a nation-state embracing the whole country. In order to achieve a smooth transition to the new system, the Emperor was moved out of Kyoto, and the Meiji revolution referred to as a revolution based on the revival of imperial rule, but it was ultimately a revolution that adapted the superstructure so as to prevent its falling behind technological developments.

It can be seen from the above that if some equilibrium is not maintained within technologies between those that are utilized for conflict (weapons) and those used in daily life (for transport, communications and production), and the former outstrips the latter, then the territory will be too large for direct rule. The country will then split up, forming small communities that will exist side by side with each other. However the relationship between these technologies and the community is not a direct one. As we shall see below, it is an indirect relationship, mediated through man-made associations.

First of all, where the level of development of technologies for daily life is low, the scale of the societies (or *Gesellschaften*) required to achieve the various goals of daily life will be commensurately small. This being the case, the people involved in them will come from a limited area, and will have little interaction with people living in other areas. This generates the principle of 'out of sight, out of mind'. There are no feelings of trust towards those from another locality, and even where there has been interaction, it is lacking in any intimacy. The community, as the unit that acts as the basis for communal living, is therefore also small. Thus the chain of causality takes the form of technology → man-made association → community society. Of course, even where the technologies for daily living lag behind those geared to warfare, as long as a territory that has expanded through military technologies brings about progress in the technologies of daily life, then the process whereby a large country breaks up into a number of small countries will not occur.

It is apparent from the above analysis that it is easy to infer what will happen in the reverse case, i.e. where the technologies for daily life are more advanced than those for warfare, or where the exercise of military technologies is restricted. Under such circumstances there are likely to be established large numbers of associations whose scope of activity is on a scale that transcends that of the contemporary nation-state. Their activities are international, and should these activities become a regular occurrence, relationships of trust will be formed between people that go beyond the confines of a single state. If these relationships are sustained, then the feelings of trust will become constant, mutual suspicion will be dispelled, and people will start to build relationships that become intimate. Moreover, with the formation of large numbers of international societies of interest, there will be mixed marriages between people from different communities, resulting in the scale of communities becoming larger. The postwar formation of the EEC in Europe, and the subsequent process of its development into the EU, can be explained in this way.

IV

We have seen above how, if we take the contemporary nation-state as our point of departure, that state can either shrink or expand depending on the nature of the relationship between military technology and technology for daily lives. Should it become too small, the state ceases to be a nation-state at all, and will probably end up as a partial nation-state, or a regional state. Similarly, if a nation-state becomes too large its very expansion is likely to undermine it, and a federation of nation-states will be produced. If either of these should happen we can no longer see them as nation-states that have expanded or contracted. They have totally changed their characters, becoming very different types of community societies.

If we apply this idea to the case of Europe, we find that for London business people, cities such as Paris and Frankfurt are closer than Manchester. The same will soon be true of Berlin and Rome. Looked at in terms of the time required for travel, the map of Europe has changed completely. In sport, too, there are now many more matches between the leading European teams, and people have become much more involved in them. Through such means the peoples of Europe are coming to share a common existence. The proposition that the peoples of Europe will belong to a single community is no longer a hollow assumption. The claim that there exist between them feelings of intimacy imbued with trust is no longer fiction, but fact.

In that sense Europeans are forming a 'European people'. Initially, however, these feelings of intimacy are very different from those that exist between, say, one English person and another. Just as until around 40–50 years ago Japanese people felt particularly at ease with others from the same hometown, so, too, are Europeans more likely to feel a special bond with someone from the same country. It is likely, therefore, that for several centuries the peoples of Europe will continue to have a dual awareness of nation.

This, however, is nothing new. Since Britain is already a union of countries under a monarchy, British people are accustomed to having two identities. One identity is as citizens of this union, the other is their identity as a member of one of the constituent nations, for example, Scotland. For many people this dual awareness causes no problem whatsoever. The most it means is supporting the country to which one belongs when there is a domestic international match, which means a match between, for example, England and Scotland. Within the European Union, however, they are coming to acquire a triple identity.

This kind of triple identity is far from unique to Britain. Many European peoples possess a triple identity within Europe. These include the Basques of Spain and the Flemish people of Belgium. For these people the formation of a 'European people' is something to be welcomed. They are happy to be dismantling the national identity that currently lies between them and Europe, and to belong directly to a

European people. This applies to Europeans of Scottish descent, for example.

On the other hand, however, there are those who feel very strongly that the absorption of nation-states into any European federation should be resisted. Many of these people are nationalists or royalists. In England this group is referred to as Eurosceptics, and the most powerful representative of this tendency is the former prime minister, Margaret Thatcher. It is not clear whether or not Lady Thatcher is a committed royalist, but what is certain is that she is a nationalist. For Lady Thatcher, opposition to European integration does not fundamentally arise from economic causes. What she finds intolerable is the possibility of European union leading to a strong pan-European representative body above the British government. Her pride will just not permit such a thing. It is just the same attitude as that of Saigo Takamori after the Meiji Restoration, who found the thought of a government in Tokyo equally hard to bear.

However, given the extent of development of technology in our daily lives and in the economy, even the Eurosceptics ultimately have no choice but to recognise some kind of federation, just as Saigo had to. If Britain were to secede from the EU, many of Britain's capitalists would immediately transfer their capital to Europe, and many of Britain's largest companies would move their head offices to Germany or France. For business people living in a world geared to the pursuit of profit such an action would be a matter of course. Failing to protect their own capital and company for reasons of patriotic sentiment, in full knowledge of the losses that they were incurring, would be conduct that disqualified them as businessmen. Since the Eurosceptics know this as well, it is impossible for them to enforce any policy in this direction. Driven on by public opinion, they chase along after the pro-European faction. The most they can do is try and resist when they think they have a strong case.

Attitudes towards any federation of nations are naturally different depending on whether a country is a republic or a monarchy. In a republic people decide on their own head of state by means of an election, so even if those who aspire to the position of head of state are unsuccessful in the election, they are likely to accept the result with a measure of tolerance, as something unavoidable. In a monarchy, however, and especially in a monarchy with a long tradition, it is not a case of anyone being able to become the monarch, but only a particular designated person. For the people of that country, for anyone else to become the monarch is inconceivable, and they would veto the idea of anyone apart from that becoming the head of state.

When Britain created the 'Commonwealth' in parallel with the British Empire, the member countries of the Commonwealth were all independent countries with their own heads of state. Despite this, Britain stipulated as an absolutely indispensable condition for its establishment that the British king or queen must be the head of the Commonwealth. There is no such condition, however, in the case of the EU. Since the British people are well aware of this, this problem is rarely discussed openly, but it is this that rankles in the hearts of royalists.

If a federation of states similar to that of Europe were to be created in Asia – what I will hereafter call an AU – this would be a major problem for some Japanese. As a result of the Pacific War Japan has already ceased to be an 'emperor system' country in the traditional sense of the phrase. Japan is a country of sovereign inhabitants, in which the emperor has no more than a symbolic role. However, what generates feelings of respect for the emperor is not his taking responsibility for political affairs as the monarch, but his symbolic role. For that reason the fact that the emperor cannot be the symbol of any 'AU' is a major problem for these people.

If Japan cannot resolve this issue before dealing with the concept of an 'Asian Union', the country at that time is likely to see the appearance not just of Asia-sceptics, but of anti-Asianists, and the result will be confusion. Should Japan remain outside any such union, the country will not be able to make sufficient use of her technology for production or the economy, and is likely to find herself isolated, resulting in enormous economic disadvantage. The then emperor will find himself caught between the 'spirits of the imperial ancestors' on the one hand, and advanced technology on the other, leading to considerable anxieties.

There is one more thing that should be re-emphasized. It is common to find in sociology the following argument. Firstly, over the course of time *Gesellschaften* gradually become stronger, and people come to act in a rational, calculated manner to achieve their objectives, so life in the country as a whole will become the life found in the big cities. People will cease to be upright, kind, sincere and possessed of a conscience, becoming calculating, selfish, hedonistic and cunning. It is not just that the strength of the *Gesellschaft* increases, but the *Gemeinschaft*, too, changes, taking on the characteristics of the *Gesellschaft*. Even the village, it is argued, will lose its characteristic virtue, and its people will become like those of the big city, living distant from and unconcerned with each other.

My own perspective, however, is rather different from this. It is a mistake to think only in terms of the most popular view, and I believe that there is one trend working in society that is likely to play a role in addition to the one mentioned in this popular view. This is the existence of the opposite tendency, namely that when a *Gesellschaft* is formed, there is also created on the basis of it a new *Gemeinschaft*. The collective ethos of the Japanese company is a conspicuous example of this, and similar tendencies can be observed to a greater or lesser extent both in the countries of Western Europe and elsewhere. A new *Gemeinschaft* formed in this way differs in character from the older type. The admired virtues are not just a revival of the older ones, but there is no doubt that for a new generation these associations do amount to places of relaxation that can give rise to feelings of intimacy imbued with trust.

For that reason a union of nations will lead to a large community transcending the nation. By contrast with the peoples of Europe, the peoples of Asia tend already to be referred to a 'the Asian people'.[3] In future the world is likely to be run on the basis of peoples in this broader sense. This perspective bears marked resemblance to Immanuel Kant's theory of peace. According to Kant people's moral development passes through three stages: lack of discipline, heteronomy (discipline by others), and autonomy. If we were to apply these three stages to a state, the period of the supremacy of the nation-state would be the first stage, i.e. lack of discipline, while the era of the United Nations would mark the period of heteronomy. During the period of heteronomy the moral laws that have to be followed by a state are imposed from outside, while in the period of autonomy moral autonomy is achieved as a result of the moral laws each individual imposes on himself or herself, with each individual enjoying absolute freedom.

If we think about things in this way, however, the issue of why a time when moral autonomy is realized should come at all – especially in the case of states – remains more or less academic. Kant failed to come up with a persuasive rational explanation as to why people might reach a point at which they can transcend nationalism, transcend federations of nations, and think of the world as a place in which they can live peacefully. Global warming is a deplorable and dangerous new phenomenon, and should act as a very stern warning to people across the globe that they should become part of a single *Gemeinschaft*. When colossal technologies transcend national boundaries, extending their benefits and disadvantages to distant lands, individuals and enterprises can no longer act purely on the basis of their own selfish interests. Their selfish acts will have to conform to a basic principle of communal living, preserving the environment for the benefit of all. The spheres where liberalism is permitted, depends upon the scale of the effectiveness of the technology that prevails. As long as each state is aware of this, the world will eventually reach Kant's period of autonomy.

V

There is a correspondence between the size of a country and the technology that is adopted. Should the technology develop so as to make a larger territorial area more appropriate, there will develop forms of economic cooperation that transcend national boundaries. Such a change in material conditions brings with it a cultural coming-together (mutual understanding) between the various peoples within the regions that are engaged in economic cooperation. Further on, this can finally bring political cooperation between them. We also have, of course, the reverse case, in which politics determines economics, which in turn gives rise to new technologies. What is important for the following discussion, however, is the first of these two cases, that is, the materialist relationship.

If we were to apply this kind of transnational trend to the case of Asia, specifically Northeast Asia we find that the concept of an Asian Union has been floated. One of the most important factors behind this idea is the relationship between Korea and Japan. Unfortunately, however, relations between the two have still not been properly recognized, and have yet to be normalised. As there has not been proper recognition of Japan's criminal and savage acts in the past, it has not been possible to conclude normal relations.

I have already discussed how close Japan and Korea used to be to each other in ancient times. As for China, Japan had long been subject to Chinese cultural tutelage through the numerous delegations sent to China. Japan was hardly ever invaded from the mainland, except for the Chinese attack at the time of the Mongol dynasty. By contrast we find Japan rampaging on the mainland at the time of Toyotomi Hideyoshi and from the Meiji period. Therefore, if Japan had had more self control, we would not have had things like the problems of the war prostitutes, or of Japan's exploitation of Koreans, nor the hatred between two peoples who are, after all, close relatives. Fourteen or fifteen centuries of history would justifiably lead one to the conclusion that Northeast Asia could be very peaceful, and hence that there is no danger of the kind of civil war we have seen in Bosnia. The proposal for a Northeast Asian community that I am going to talk about below is therefore far from being just a dream. At first glance it may seem to be so because the Japanese have little enthusiasm for that kind of idea, and the reason for this lack of enthusiasm is that there still exist among Japanese feelings of discrimination in relation to Asia. Japanese who believe that it is possible for it to form a community with Pacific Caucasian countries such as America, Canada, Australia and New Zealand, but not with the countries of Asia, do so because they have in their hearts latent feelings of contempt towards Asia. This attitude results in their feeling that it is not possible for Japan to participate in any kind of Northeast Asian Economic Community (NEAC). If there is to be such participation, the Japanese themselves have to sort out Japan's past, and that can only happen if there is a thoroughgoing debate on it among the Japanese people themselves.

During the Pacific War Japan advocated what was called the Greater East Asian Co-Prosperity Sphere. My idea of an NEAC is very different from this. The Co-Prosperity Sphere presupposed and justified Japanese domination in Asia, and so an absolute condition for its existence was a Japanese monopoly in the political and military spheres. However, the assembly of any NEAC – and even if it was just an economic community it would have to have some kind of decision-making body, i.e. an assembly, given that it would be making decisions independently of the national governments – would not be mono-polized by any one country.

As has been reiterated, the war-time predecessor of the NEAC, i.e. the Greater East Co-Prosperity Sphere was very discriminative, as Japan at that time was supposed to assign to the member countries a colonial status. Obviously, we should not repeat the same mistake. No member country of the NEAC should dominate over others in the assemblies of the community. However, in the case of Asia it would not be possible to adopt the democratic method of allocating the seats in accordance with the size of the population. The reason for this is that if this happened the fate of all proposals made in the assembly would end up being determined according to the wishes of China, and this would result in all the other countries withdrawing from the union. This is the reason why I propose that each member countries is divided into an appropriate number of constituencies, with each constituency having equal representation. The number of constituencies may differ from one country to another, but they are decided such that the equality of the constituencies is respected by all member countries.

However, Northeast Asian community cannot adopt the same economic principles as the EEC. In the case of the EEC the level of economic development of the member countries was in all cases relatively high, so the basic principles have been those of free competition and the removal of economic barriers. Within any NEAC, however, there will exist very large areas that were economically relatively backward, and these areas will have to be protected. Within these areas unlimited freedom must not be given to the non-NEAC members, nor is it possible even for the member countries of the NEAC freely to promote economic development in these backward areas. Development theories tell us that what is likely to be necessary is the careful development of industry in the more backward areas; this programme is designed and implemented by the headquarters of the NEAC.

As for the more developed areas, the community should more or less follow along the lines of the EEC, they should not adopt a fortress mentality either in their relationships within the community, nor with those nations outside it. Since the purpose of the community is economic development, it needs to be sensitive to technological developments in countries outside the community, and for that reason it is absolutely essential that the doors of the community always remain open as wide as possible.

However, if there was at a stroke an across the board liberalization of industry, some industries in some countries would probably be in danger of being wiped out. This could happen in any of the member countries. For a certain number of years after the establishment of any NEAC, cooperation between the various member countries is particularly important. For that reason the community will not embrace completely free competition, but even so commerce between the various member countries will increase considerably over and above that which existed prior to the establishment of the community. I should also reiterate that as far as relations with countries outside are concerned, a greater openness than currently exists should be established as the basic principle under normal circumstances, particularly after the initial period of a few years is passed.

In a community such as an NEAC that is made up of countries with different levels of development, it is essential that there be strict monitoring of qualifications should an enterprise wish to expand its operations to another country, in order to prevent the economic exploitation of one member country by another. First, it should be obligatory for employees to own shares in the company that is moving in, and enterprises that are not willing to adhere to this rule should not be permitted to set up operations in this way. That is to say, they have to allow employees to become shareholders of the company that employs them. If companies have to lend their new employees the capital required to purchase the shares, then the arrival of enterprises from other member countries will tend to contribute to the development of that nation's capital. Since in any case the amount of capital that has to be advanced is limited to this specified amount, it will not be a particular burden on the enterprise that is moving in. Where Japanese enterprises, for example, extend their operations to another member country in this way, the Japanese enterprise will have access to the local labour force, and the locality will obtain capital. Of course if funds are advanced free of charge, the net profits of the incoming enterprise will be reduced by the amount equal to the interest on the funds that have been advanced, but this amount, or some part of it, can surely be borne as development assistance for the NEAC.

I think that this kind of socialist consideration based on the favourable treatment of the employee is essential, given that the regions into which the enterprises are advancing are in need of development, and these regions also tend to belong to countries where we have capitalism from above, although they are invariably referred to as socialist. This is because if enterprises were to move in in their purely capitalist form, the capitalist country would end up exploiting the developing region; the former must, therefore, support the latter by some way like this or other.

I have written earlier that any NEAC must start off as a railway-based community whose main constituent is Japan's *Shinkansen* (Bullet Train) lines. Railways are a basic industry, and earlier on other industries utilised railways to engage in economic development, but the level of development achieved by railways per se is very high. This includes direct and indirect effects. As a matter of fact, the existence of railways can make a great difference to the possibility of other industries being able to develop. Railways are likely to be greatly appreciated by the actual countries in which they are constructed. Especially when the rolling stock operating on the railway is that of the *Shinkansen*, and it can carry freight on the same scale and the same speed as the *Shinkansen*, the economic frontier in the remoter parts of the hinterland could be opened up considerably. The operating technology of Japan's *Shinkansen*, moreover, is second to none in the world. There is no reason to shut that technology up within the Japanese archipelago. Just as in the contemporary world we have an economic community based on the jet aeroplane, so we can have a community based on the *Shinkansen*. It is possible for there to be a mutual distribution of benefits, in the same way that America's aeroplane companies make a profit by providing the planes, and individual countries benefit from having air services at the level of America's. Similar things should and would happen in NEAC.

The same is true of roads. The electric power industry can also be a basic industry that can make a big contribution to the economy. With the establishment of an electric power industry both agriculture and the villages' capacity for manufacturing could improve remarkably. The provision of waterways would enable the operation of very large scale agriculture in some regions of China. Not only would farmers use tractors but they would also travel to work in the agricultural areas each day by car. Output of agricultural products would increase remarkably, and the cost of foodstuffs would be dramatically reduced. Agricultural development in the remoter regions would encourage production of the consumer goods required by those regions, absorbing the surplus population of the agricultural villages. Development in the more backward regions of China would certainly be accompanied by major developments in the economy of China as a whole. Whatever happens, though, it must be up to the headquarters of the NEAC to use the fruits of investment that has materialised from the NEAC, in a way such that they would contribute to a further big development of the region.

What I have described above are somewhat textbook-type policies for the development of backward areas, but they would easily become possible if NEAC countries were to come together and cooperate as a community. Most of the fruits of this cooperation would accrue to the backward areas where investment took place, while the remainder would be returned to the country that had furnished the capital. Large areas of territory that had lain idle purely because they possessed no capital, would be put to use and become active through cooperation between the various member countries. Agricultural development in this kind of backward region would then push petty agriculture in Japan and Korea towards the production of higher quality goods, which is what has happened in the agricultural regions of northern Italy (for example the Alba region).

During the sixteenth and seventeenth centuries Asian trade was conducted in a semi-inland sea whose outer bound was the sea routes connecting Japan, the Ryukyu Islands, Taiwan, the Philippines and Indonesia, and the inner one the coastal route along the Asian mainland from Singapore to Pusan. When the hinterlands experienced increased activity, the same was naturally true of the semi-inland sea. This sea area did not just link the northern and southern parts of East Asia. Through Singapore it was linked to the West, with India and Europe, and to the south towards Australia. It goes without saying that through Japan it could extend eastwards towards America, and from Korea northwards into Siberia and Russia. Of course, Japan is the leading candidate to play a major role in this plan; in spite of their being in such an advantageous position, Japan's political leaders have done nothing to make a significant contribution to the programme described.

I must emphasize that the development of East Asia necessitates the utilization of the semi-inland sea described above, while conversely any successful reactivation of the semi-inland sea will link its hinterlands to markets in other parts of the world. For that reason it is necessary to construct modern port facilities in appropriate locations both on the outer and inner perimeters of the semi-inland sea. It goes without saying that a NEAC would have to have a modern fleet of large merchant ships. Fortunately any NEAC would include Japan and Korea, both of which are major shipping nations, and so it would not be difficult to ply the semi-inland sea with large numbers of modern ships. This would in addition stimulate anew the economic development of both countries.

Thought about in this way it is clear that a NEAC would be very different in character from the EEC. The main purpose of the EEC is to integrate the markets of the individual countries by removing the national boundaries between the different countries, and to utilize for reproduction the benefits of the larger market that results from this. By contrast an NEAC would basically be a community whose prime purpose was economic construction. Of course, if that economic construction were successful an expanded market would come into being of its own accord. Without that building up, however, the market would not exist, even though all the boundaries are entirely removed.

Construction is, however, possible. In East Asia there is a skewed distribution of resources, labour, capital and technology between the different countries. No single one of these countries, therefore, is in the position of being able to push forward the construction on its own. Cooperation, however, would immediately provide the elements essential for construction, and so such construction is an endogenous possibility within the NEAC. To cooperate in this way, and create a community, is a basic condition of endogenous economic growth. For that reason it is essential that the headquarters of the NEAC possesses the ability to draw up detailed plans for more effective growth.

This does not mean that the NEAC countries as a body would be run along the lines of a planned economy. What sort of projects should be promoted by the NEAC headquarters, and in which regions, should be determined by the community authorities following consultation between the different countries. Once these projects have been decided on, the implementation process should be entrusted to private enterprises in each country, who act in accordance with market principles. Moreover, if there is an information network that covers northeast Asia as a whole, contacts between the different private enterprises and the NEAC headquarters are likely to much more effective. However, because such a procedure could result in the enrichment of some member countries and the impoverishment of others, it remains imperative that there should be some consideration of how the rights and benefits of each project should be fairly redistributed among different regions. Such a procedure would minimise the possibility of unfair treatment of regions and countries. For example, the practice that I mentioned above of introducing a system of employee shareholding, and advancing capital wherewith to purchase those shares, is one means of distributing the returns justly. In terms of any discussion of economic systems, an NEAC would probably be a hybrid of a planned economy and a free enterprise system.

Such a work of construction is bound to take time, with only part of the projects being brought into being each year. The results, therefore, would also not appear all at once. With several decades of consolidation, however, it will become apparent that there is a big difference between the situation with a NEAC, and one without it. The price of foodstuffs would be much cheaper, which would in turn inhibit rises in real wages, while the international competitiveness of the NEAC countries *vis-à-vis* those outside would have been greatly improved.

Let me finally say something about the relationship between my NEAC and the APEC (the Asia-Pacific Economic Cooperation organization). APEC is a loose regional consultative body aimed at regional cooperation. It is a forum at which America argues for liberalisation of trade and investment, and Japan asserts her claims for special measures to be applied to the rice trade. Assertions of this kind by both countries are mistaken. In economic terms Japan possesses a comparative disadvantage in the production of rice. Since this is unlikely in the near future to change to a position of comparative advantage, this cannot be said to be a case of an infant industry, in the sense implied by trade theory and development theory. There is no economic foundation, therefore, for protecting Japan's rice production. However, to implement the total liberalisation called for by America, with no exceptions whatsoever, would kill in their infancy the infant industries in the true sense of the word that are dotted throughout the Asian countries. If investment, too, is driven by the profit motive, specifically the short term profit motive of America, there will be no investment in the industries that are really essential to the economic development of Asia. The basic foundations for that development will end up not being constructed, and Asia will be devastated by the irresponsible enterprises and capital of the advanced countries.

By contrast, a NEAC would have the objective of establishing the basic foundations for development. For that purpose, as I have stated repeatedly, cooperation is essential, and the member states must work together to produce the best possible plans. At the stage of implementing these plans market principles will be introduced. Plans will be implemented by enterprises in competition with each other. However, not to have such planning, giving free rein to the market and abandoning the economy to *laissez-faire*, would in effect consign the developing economies to the exploitation of the more advanced economies. The first thing that must be done is to establish the NEAC. The liberalization advocated by America at APEC will come afterwards.

VI

The NEAC would be an economic community, and not a political community, nor a cultural community. Questions of politics or culture, therefore, will not be dealt with directly by the NEAC. However, just as the success of the EEC gave rise to the EU, so too, if the NEAC is successful, it may well expand into a composite community embracing sectors well outside those that it started with (for example railway or shipping cooperation). This may fully be expected soon to bring its development into a stronger, more inclusive community.

There were many drafts of the Greater East Asian Co-Prosperity Sphere, but the right-wing version subscribed to by the military made mistakes even in the cultural sphere by trying to use Japanese culture to control the other member countries. Since the Co-Prosperity Sphere was an imperialist community, the Japanese thought that Japan had to be the leader of East Asia, and so the religion and culture of that leader must have a higher standing within the Co-Prosperity Sphere. Everywhere occupied by Japan, *torii* (ceremonial gates for Shinto shrines) were set up and shrines established, and the inhabitants were made to worship in the direction of Tokyo. Even supposing that Japanese at the time believed that if such a childish ritual was imposed on the people it would soon turn to heartfelt worship and faith, this was an excessively simple view. The only thing that results from coercion is antagonism and resistance. This error on the part of Japan must be made to serve as a warning to the countries within the NEAC. No country should think that its own religion and ideology are superior. They may happen currently to be appropriate to some countries and not to other countries, and just because they suit one country must not lead one to think that they are suited to others.

Similarly it is not a question of which countries' living styles and decorum are good, and which bad. People should also be free to follow the etiquette and customs of countries outside the community. When the community comes to have a long history, the customs and etiquette of the member countries are likely to synthesize with each other, perhaps producing customs and practices characteristic to the community, and common to all its members. Such developments should, however, always occur naturally. There is no question of their being produced according to some plan or intention. Whether they happen or not will depend on future generations which are as yet unborn. All we can do is receive the diversity of the present. Similarly culture as a whole is multifaceted. In the case of the NEAC, however, all the member countries share some similarities in terms of culture and practices, and so it is hard to think of this as a region likely to experience major problems of cultural friction or clashes between different practices.

Concerning other aspects, however, there is likely to appear uniformity and standardization within the community. For example, in Japan the railways have high platforms as we have in Britain, whereas in Korea and China they have low platforms of the kind found in America and continental Europe. Where stations deal with international trains the platforms will all have to be of the same type. Unless this is done there will be the trouble of building rolling stock that can be used with both types of platform. (Fortunately Japan is an island country, so the country's *Shinkansen* will not need to be used intact on the mainland.) There will be many other commodities, too, that will certainly have to be standardized.

Education, including areas like training in manufacturing and administrative techniques, will also have to be brought in line. An NEAC is bound to need large numbers of administrators. If these officials do not have common administrative techniques, it will be impossible for them to work together. In order to achieve this there will have to be established in several locations within the community centres whose function will be to train administrators for the NEAC. Both staff and students of these centres will be international. Where officials are involved in technology, they will also need to be trained in most advanced technologies.

We are fortunate in that the quality and education level of the people living within the NEAC area are not much behind that of the populations of any other area of the world at the present time. Moreover, we may say that further provision of education could provide a large amount of high quality human capital relatively easily.

It is crucial, however, that the realm of education does not become dominated by what we might refer to as 'bad money drives out good'. There will need to be some equalization between the standards in higher education in the different countries, and the establishment of a system where one diploma is equivalent to another. We cannot allow people to obtain employment with the NEAC on the basis of university qualifications in a country where it is easier to achieve such qualifications than elsewhere.

Once the standardization of school and college education in the different countries has been achieved, it will be possible to open up the labour markets of the individual countries. Even if labour is granted the freedom to move, and permitted to work in other member countries than their own, workers will not be discriminated against in the market on the basis of nationality. Under such circumstances countries will no longer be able to engage in trade on the strength of cheap labour. This is because a homogeneous and mobile labour force means that workers in all countries will be of the same ability, and so wage levels will equalize out. For such a situation to come about, however, it is likely to take 60 or 70 years. The urban areas of China, as well as Taiwan and Korea, are likely to catch up Japan very quickly in this respect, whereas for the Chinese hinterland it will take somewhat longer.

As for relative wages, wages for workers in Japan will have to fall. However, as it is expected that a significant part of orders made by the NEAC will go to Japan, it is very likely that Japan will be able to break out of the deadlock that its economy finds itself in today. Those who will gain the most benefit, however, will be the inhabitants of the hinterland areas, obviously because such a development would transform their unutilized resources into actual economic resources. Along with the progress of such development would come equalization in the per capita income of the countries of Northeast Asia.

At some stage in this process tariffs within the community would be completely abolished. Just as the internal border posts that existed in feudal Japan are now regarded as a complete mistake, so too would tariffs end up being seen as something almost incomprehensible. The abolition of tariffs for trade within an area brings about a great expansion in that community's trade. Developments of this kind have already been proved in the case of the EEC, and once there is a lively exchange of commodities and people there are also cultural exchanges. The result of this is that cultures start to merge, and to become more uniform.

Other things would come along with this. People would naturally intermarry with each other. There are no fundamental major physical differences between the peoples of Northeast Asia, and they can in a broad sense be regarded as part of the same race, so international marriages between those from different countries can easily take place. The extent of such intermarriage would be likely to increase considerably. International marriage also deepens mutual understanding of people's customs and codes of conduct. This in its turn would start to make culture more mixed, breaking down the barriers imposed hitherto by national consciousness. Along with this would come a heightened awareness of being a broader 'people' embracing all the peoples of Northeast Asia, what Takata Yasuma referred to as the East Asian people (*Toa minzoku*). In this way the economic community (*Gesellschaft*) of the NEAC would prepare the way for a community society (*Gemeinschaft*) of the Northeast Asian people.

An economic community is a society of interest (or profit), more specifically brought together in the mutual pursuit of advantage. It is a means of competing to obtain advantage, and people will discard their friends, switching to new, more advantageous friends, where it is to their greater advantage to do so. A society of interest operates rationally; it is a man-made body, whose members are shrewd operators. However, should the members of a society of interest become related to each other by blood, however, those members can no longer operate purely on the basis of gain, introducing into that society of interest elements other than profit, such as duty, obligation and love.

The economic society that comes into being within a single nation state is in that sense a somewhat imperfect society of interest. Yet, an international economic society consisting of different peoples would be in this sense a rather 'purer' society of interest. The economic society resulting from the creation of an NEAC would initially be a relatively pure society of interest, but with increasing intermarriage people would over time increasingly become part of a single, broader people, and as people began to be aware of this the level of purity would decline. Just as the society of interest within the nation-state has become a society of interest based on a people, i.e. a community-type society of interest, so, too, would the NEAC start off purely as a society of interest, and eventually develop into a community-type society of interest.

A transformation of this kind is hardly surprising, and occurs frequently. As I have already noted, mainland Britain is inhabited by the English, Scottish and Welsh. The relationships between them were initially those of conqueror and conquered, but most of them now all see themselves as British (those who live in the British Isles). The country that these peoples have formed – the United Kingdom – is the nation-state of the British in this broader sense. This means that commerce between them due to their self-interest has generated in them a common sense of identity as British. This demonstrates that while societies of interest can be formed on the basis of the community known as the nation, we also have the reverse situation whereby a community in the form of a more extended people is created on the basis of a society of interest such as the NEAC.

Once the NEAC has developed to this level it is likely to start dissolving to form an NEAU (Northeast Asian Union). It is not just economic aspects that the countries of Northeast Asia will have in common. They will have a great deal of other things in common too. At this stage functions undertaken independently by the individual member states, with the exception of things like policing and defence, are likely to become effectively redundant.

For example, the major economic functions undertaken by the state are the implementation of taxation and monetary policy, but once the peoples of the NEAC start to think of themselves as part of a single broader people the different countries will no longer cling to having their own separate currency systems. This is because having a single currency throughout the whole NEAC territory will bring greater stability to currency values than a situation where each country has its own currency would produce. It will also be more appropriate to the formulation of rational economic plans. Currency union has been opposed by parts of the EU, in particular the Thatcherites in Britain, but this is more of an emotional reaction. If we look at Japan, it is apparent that dealing with the currencies issued by the various domains at the time of the Meiji Restoration required considerable efforts, but they were unified into the single currency of the new Meiji government relatively easily. In just the same way, currency union is not an impossibly difficult thing in economic terms. Moreover, the fact that a single currency system can do no harm is true not just of market-based communities, but also of communities whose purpose is construction, where the growth rates of the developed member countries are lower than those of the developing member countries.

Since public investment policy and large scale investments are all carried out by the NEAC, the matters dealt with by the governments of the individual countries will be confined to those that are relatively small scale. In this respect the relationship between the headquarters of the NEAC and the individual country governments will resemble those that exist at present between the central and local governments within each country. Moreover the governments of the individual countries will no longer be able to have a totally free hand even in relation to decisions on small-scale investment. This is because if there are too many small scale investments taking place in parallel with the NEAC's large scale investments, this will result in inflation, reducing the utility of the investments of both the NEAC and the individual countries. The individual country governments will have to conduct their fiscal and investment policies with constant reference to the NEAC.

With free mobility within the region, and a unified currency, it will no longer be possible for the governments of the separate countries to possess independence and autonomy in the setting of taxes. If one country should reduce the level of income tax, for example, the people who live in the countries where income tax levels are now proportionately higher will probably start to migrate to the country where the level is lower. This will lead to a chorus of criticism of this country's apparent attempt to make itself into a tax haven. Ultimately there will be no alternative but to raise and lower the income tax levels of the various countries in step with each other, and it will be impossible for any of the national governments to demonstrate their individuality.

The same is true of commodity taxes. If a country's commodity taxes are low there will be substantial exports of those goods to that country. The consumers of all the other countries will go there to purchase those goods, with a view to reducing their payments of consumption taxes. This means that decisions on commodity tax rates will not be a purely domestic question, but one concerning all the member countries. This matter too, therefore, will become one on which a single country can no longer make decisions by itself, but will require the consent of countries across the region.

With autonomous decision-making on monetary and fiscal policy becoming impossible in this way, the sovereignty of the various member countries will have become like an empty shell. Of course the individual governments will have to communicate the wishes of their country through the representatives they send to the NEAC, and so countries will retain their national institutions for making decisions and implementing them, such as their parliaments and administrative machinery. The number of issues dealt with by those institutions, however, will decrease compared with the present, and are likely to become far more simple in content. Moreover with the transformation of the NEAC into the NEAU, a large part of the world will be embraced by the EU, the NEAU and other federations of nations. The United Nations is likely no longer be the union of states that it is today, but a union of federations of states.

My own belief is that when this happens we will tend to find that disputes between the various federations of states will be solved not through the use of force, but by negotiation. It will be impossible for the NEAU to carry out on other federations of states surprise attacks of the kind made at Pearl Harbor. A third federation of states would be bound to play the role of mediator, while countries within the NEAU would be divided over whether to support or oppose such action. An autocratic system of rule, like that of Japan's emperor system or that of Germany or Italy at the time of the Second World War, would probably become impossible. If my hypothesis were to prove correct, the federations of states would no longer need military capability for protection against attacks by other federations, or for attacking other federations. The armed forces of a federation would tend to become police reserves in that they would act to supplement the police forces. Once this happened the spirit of the Japanese constitution, with its rejection of force as a means of solving international disputes, would no longer be just an ideal, but a reality.

Even so, disputes might occur within the NEAU itself, and solving these disputes might require the use of force. If member states handed over their national forces to the NEAU at the time of its formation, then the NEAU government would have a monopoly of force within the federation, and the government's use of force internally would not be an act of war, but a simple act of policing. Of course there could be civil wars such as arose in Bosnia, but historical experience suggests that we can be fairly optimistic that in the case of Northeast Asia complex and persistent civil conflict is unlikely to occur. Moreover, as we have seen in the case of Bosnia, once military force has been embarked on there are likely to be continuing parallel efforts to reach a peace agreement, minimizing the extent of conflict. In the era of federations of states the total war waged during the twentieth century by nation states will come to be regarded as anomalous and inconceivable. Even though some of the countries of the NEAU may be communist, and others monarchies, this distinction that is valid now is likely to have very little real significance in the future. The era of nation states will have come to an end, and we will have embarked on an era of a much larger state, what would perhaps be called a United States of Northeast Asia (USNEA).

Lecture 3
The Dawn of Asia

Whatever country we look at, we find that in ancient times the imperial or royal family was dominant in economic terms, while the economy of the common people was so weak that it could be virtually disregarded. Over time the royal economy was first of all rationalized, and then consciously operated along capitalist lines. This led to the appearance of countries of capitalism from above in which political power played an important role. In colonies such as America and Canada, however, the colonies themselves had long lacked any great influence, and the colonists, who had no political power, worked to build up their own private economies. This led to the formation of a macro economy characterized by mutual competition between a large number of private enterprises, i.e. capitalism from below. Looking at the main industrial countries now such as those belonging to G.7 or G.8, it is only America and Canada that can be characterized in this way. For a country of capitalism from above to make the transition to becoming one of capitalism from below, there has to be a democratic tradition that will protect these small private economies. Only Britain has that kind of long democratic tradition. Britain early on created a structure that would limit the economic activities of the royal family in the form of a parliament, and its macro-economy was soon successful in making the transition to capitalism from below. France is another example of the capitalist economy starting from above and transforming itself so as to include enterprises from below within it, through successive revolutions for democracy. By contrast other long-established countries like Japan, Germany and Italy, where the progress of democracy was delayed, all managed to establish unified nation states in the period 1861–71, and only then were they eventually successful in becoming second generation capitalist countries, strongly characterized by capitalism from above.

In countries of this kind, however, there were huge differentials between those private economies that were linked to political influence, and the very small private economies that were distinct from it. This resulted in a movement to eradicate these differentials. Where the movement was led by socialists this pointed to a socialist or communist country, and where a movement was led by nationalists, the direction was that of absolutism, fascism and nazism. Countries in the latter group that were defeated in the Second World War reverted to capitalism from above, while China after the war took the path of socialism. The road to pure socialism is, however, rough, almost, one could say, impossible. This is firstly because mutual competition between small enterprises is prohibited, and secondly because abstinence is demanded of government leaders. Abstinence is possible in the short term, but over the longer term it is extremely difficult to continue with total uprightness. Once a government ceases to be stoical the result is socialist exploitation. On the other hand, if people are forbidden to engage in competition, the operation of private economies becomes irresponsible. Socialist countries therefore at some stage have to permit competition between private economies, and in order to do that they have to provide people with the opportunity of making a profit. Since it is state-owned enterprises that offer most of the opportunities for profit-acquisition, a key question is how state-owned enterprises should be privatized, and what sort of state-owned enterprises should not be privatized, but rather retained under the aegis of the state. If they are, indeed, to be sold off, there is also the problem of choosing whom they should be handed over to. Any disposition of the national assets that entails selling them off to some evil individual devoid of any patriotism could invite national ruin. Even if the individual were upright, he or she might be lacking in ability, which would mean that a carefully nurtured state-owned enterprise might come to naught. China can now be said to be entering this kind of crucial period.

Japan, too, earlier experienced such a period. The Tokugawa *Bakufu* fell in 1867, and from around 1870 the new government started protecting and fostering industry. The companies supported by the government (capitalism from above) developed markedly, but over the course of time their operating situation deteriorated, because they constantly set wages at a high level in order to demonstrate the prestige of the new government. From around 1880 the government started to sell off its assets, and by 1884 privatization was being undertaken, with the sale of government enterprises. At a stroke the private sector individuals who had acquired the enterprises became extremely rich. The state enterprises were technological leaders, and their capital equipment was also very modern by comparison with that of enterprises in the private sector, so it was not at all hard to achieve immense profits through operating them. The purchasers of these state enterprises were constantly camped in the vicinity of the government, in the hope of receiving yet more favours. It was this that enabled the collusion between the government and the *zaibatsu*. The original version of the government–business–bureaucracy complex that has been so famous in Japan, and has now become notorious, was thus formed through the sale of government assets in the early Meiji period.

Similarly Prime Minister Margaret Thatcher acquired a large number of supporters through selling off council houses at knock down prices. Thus a state's withdrawal from industry is far from meaning a retreat on the part of the government. It brings instead a broadening of the base of government. Seizing control of anything and everything is a dangerous policy for a government, for if any single thing falls into difficulties the government finds itself the target of criticism. When state assets are to be sold off, however, the government has to bear in mind that any purchaser is likely to become a future supporter of the government, and ensure as far as possible that the sale is to an able and trustworthy individual. In China the term 'socialism with Chinese characteristics' is currently used, but I think of it as a form of what I have referred to as capitalism from above.

It is of course true that there are, in a socialist economy, some sectors that have to be placed under the control of the government. First of all there are the economic activities of the government sector itself. Having a government that is not going to collapse is a fundamental human right of a people, and if the government is made too extravagant, sustaining it will soon become very difficult. For that reason both government and government offices have to be as humble as possible. There is a tendency in both socialist and capitalist countries for government buildings to be constructed rather lavishly, and such things should be more modest. The level of welfare that the government offers to the people, too, should not be too high. Of course, if the level is too low the government might as well give up providing any welfare whatsoever, so deciding on the appropriate level is very difficult. Care therefore has to be paid in determining the level of welfare, bearing in mind what can be supported by the current state of the national economy. All individuals wishing to receive welfare over and above that level will have to make additional payments. The welfare received by people depends on the total welfare provided by the government, and where this is distributed between individuals according to need, the government must not show any favouritism towards particular individuals. There are, however, cases where individuals or enterprises claim that the decisions of the government are unjust and discriminatory towards them. In Japan the *zaibatsu* were always favourably treated. This provoked anti-*zaibatsu* and anti-government sentiments among the people. On the other hand having a group of *zaibatsu* loyal to the government can be extremely important in supporting government moves to develop the national economy. The major problem in starting with an economy in which a group of *zaibatsu* and private enterprises receives favourable treatment from the government, however, is how to make a smooth transition to an economy that is equitable towards all individuals and enterprises. Japan has been at a loss as to how to achieve this transition, and still is. It is a problem that is likely to become serious for China as well in the future.

For such a transition to be successful, democracy must have developed to the extent that people below can resist pressures from above. This was a process that even in Britain took a long time. In this case the operating costs of the monarchy and government budgets eventually came to require the approval of parliament, and these tasks became in the process an important part of the work of parliament. In this sense parliamentary democracy in Britain had the task of restraining the powers of the king. This is a point of major difference between countries with a long history, and the countries of the New World. In China there exist circumstances that are also found in the countries of Europe, with their long traditions, but which have not existed in America. America needs to recognise to some extent the particular circumstances of China, without thinking of China as a communist version of Asiatic despotism because of its tardiness in making the transition to capitalism from below. China has to strive for the early achievement of democracy without presuming upon that understanding. A public declaration of the appointed time would also be likely to enhance China's international standing.

It was Hegel who initiated the tradition whereby the peoples of Europe regarded the Chinese emperor as a despot. Marx, who was strongly influenced by Hegel, devised the concept of a substructure that he called 'the Asiatic mode of production' in an attempt to provide a materialist explanation – i.e. an explanation in terms of the mode of production – for the superstructure he identified as 'Asiatic despotism'. According to Marx the Asiatic mode of production was based on natural conditions in Asia that were quite different from those that existed in Europe. Both in India and in China there were vast tracts of land, crossed by huge rivers. This meant that flood control and irrigation had long been operations of major importance in these countries. Land that benefited from these works gained in value, while land that did not benefit in this way was lacking in value. Those who carried out these works naturally became the landlords. Flood control and irrigation, however, needed large amounts of labour, meaning that the work could only be carried out by the very largest landlords. The ruler did not just use the people to fight his wars for him. He was also able to use them to furnish the materials for daily existence. A relationship based on obedience to orders, of the kind found in the armed forces, thus also prevailed outside the military sphere, in the realm of daily life. It was therefore natural that Asian monarchs should be autocrats.

This view of China put forward by Marx had a conspicuous influence on research on China by later Marxist scholars, of whom Karl A. Wittfogel is particularly significant. Wittfogel was a student of Max Weber. From 1925 to 1933 he worked at a research institute in Frankfurt, where he focussed his attention on the study of China. In this work he sought to explain from a Marxist perspective how the autocratic bureacratic rule that existed in China resulted from the large scale flood control works carried out by the state. Of course it has been possible for there to exist within China itself views of China that are very different from this kind of Hegelian or Marxian perspective. For example, in AD 587 at the time of the Sui dynasty in China, a system of qualifying examinations for those who wished to become high ranking state officials was enacted. Up until that time the selection of government officials had been carried out in accordance with the rule whereby emphasis was placed on virtuous conduct. However, because this system favoured the privileged nobility class, under the Sui there was a change to a system of higher civil service examinations to select officials objectively on the basis of their ability through fair examinations. This marked an attempt in China at that time to appoint the personnel within the government – which at the time meant the court – in accordance with efficiency and individualism; that is to say, ranking of officers at court was determined not by lineage but by ability, and in accordance with objective fact in the form of examination results, rather than according to the wishes of emperor or senior officials. This suggests that far from being an Asiatic despot, the Chinese emperor should have been thought of as one of the world's leading democrats. Viewed from this perspective, any depiction of China as an absolutist state resting on an 'Asiatic mode of production' must be said to be a long way from the truth. On the other hand I have taken the view that the superstructure of Japan is in Marxian terms despotic, while its substructure is certainly not Marxist because of Asiatic-type natural endowments of vast tracts of territory crossed by great river are not available in Japan. This means that Japan's superstructure does not correspond to its substructure. This fact would appear to make Japan a counterexample not just to Marx's Asiatic mode of production, but to a materialist view of history.

What may be even more difficult for Marxists is that it was the emperor of Japan who was the despot in Asia. Because both the kingdom of Wa and the kingdom of Nihon sent emissaries to the Sui court, the fact that China had introduced a system of higher civil service examinations was almost certainly well known in the Japanese archipelago. As I have already mentioned, however, Nihon sought to establish a country where there could be no revolution, and so tried to consolidate the position of the ruling class at court and in government. The government of the time decreed the status of each family line, and made court or government appointments dependent on status. Right through until the end of the Tokugawa period Japan resolutely refused to introduce a Chinese-type examination system. In Japan the achievement of high political position depended either on being born into a family of noble lineage, or on the bestowing of special favour by the ruler. It was impossible to achieve distinction as a government official through an impartial examination open to people as a whole. Japan's national polity was built on the basis of this rejection of higher civil service examinations. The words of Hegel which I cited at the end of my first lecture have in recent times been more applicable to Japan than to China. That the destruction of the Qing dynasty meant that China was one step ahead of Japan in having a republican government must be regarded as natural. Unfortunately, however, the potentially democratic system of higher civil service examinations had been abolished towards the end of the dynasty in 1904, and was not revived in the subsequent period of the Chinese republic, with its expectations of democracy in the wake of the abolition of the monarchy. In order to resolve this superficial contradiction, we need to discuss the issue in a little more detail.

The system of higher civil service examinations was a good one. It was democratic, and gave everyone a chance. This meant that those with ability posed a challenge to the examinations, which resulted in their becoming more difficult, and the questions became harder and harder. Questions were proposed in an attempt to catch out candidates, and so passing the examinations required a certain technique. Thus passing the examinations did not necessarily mean that appropriate people had been chosen to become officials. Every time poor quality officials appeared the examination system was subject to criticism. This led to growing demands for philosopher-politics, with politics being conducted by those outstanding in intellect and cultivation, and in consequence the examination questions became increasingly detached from the concerns of the real world. Thus, while the education received by those who were successful in the examinations was aimed at encouraging the literary and the artistic, it eventually became useless for a politician. The higher civil service examinations ended up choosing the wrong people. Moreover, as the examinations got more difficult, they were increasingly attended by impropriety. It was not just the candidates who acted dishonestly, but the examiners, too, were also prone to partiality in their scrutiny. Even worse, some of those failing the examinations even led rebellions against the authorities. The whole process ended in the abolition of the examinations system, but by that time it was already too late, and the Qing dynasty was unable to prevent its own downfall. So a system that at first sight appears ideal can be seen on consideration to have been quite the opposite, bringing only decline.

The examinations system also made China into a country ruled by the literati. This was because the examinations used to choose civil officials were more difficult than those used in the selection of military officials, so civil officials had a higher status. This led in the second half of the nineteenth century to China's becoming a country where military considerations were subordinate to civil ones. Civil officials had no interest in military affairs. This resulted not only in China's becoming weak in terms of military provision, but also failing to provide the foundations for modern industry. At the same time Japan was a country controlled by military officials, with almost all the civil officials of the early Meiji period being former *samurai*, and so in Japan modern industries developed rapidly. It was not surprising that in the Sino-Japanese War of 1894–95 the great country of China should have been defeated by the small country of Japan. Now, however, following Japan's defeat in the Second World War, Japan has thrown away its armaments, and in China the top leadership of the Chinese Communist Party consists of university science graduates. Among Japan's political leadership there are hardly any individuals with a scientific background. Any comparison between China and Japan of the relative status of civil and military officials shows a complete inversion of the earlier position. While this remains to be a disparity in military power it causes no great problem, but if the effect extends to modern industries, it is China that in the future is likely to become the leading industrial power in Asia. However, causation in history is very subtle, and it is a mistake to read history carelessly.

II

In addition to this, there is the analysis of China from a 'spiritualistic' – or rather neo-spiritualistic – perspective developed by Max Weber. In China there were from ancient times two religions. One was Taoism, the other Confucianism. Taoism was a religion indigenous to China itself. It was a mystic religion, deeply concerned with people's lives, souls and deaths, and with life after death. Confucianism, by contrast, was concerned with the mundane, with relations between one person and another, and the rules governing people's lives. Rather than a religion, it was more an ethic, or moral philosophy. According to Weber the conflict between Taoism and Confucianism was a struggle by each side to gain the support of the emperor and the imperial court. Confucianism traditionally was on the side of the government, and the tenets of Confucianism continued to be the principles behind the imperial administration. China was a country where dynasties continued to change as a result of revolutions, but despite these changes of dynasty China consistently remained a Confucian state. The imperial court, however, almost always professed Taoism. The Chinese imperial court was a large one consisting of the empress and large numbers of concubines, attended by many maidservants and eunuchs, and so the court could become a major locus of resistance to the government. This scenario continued for the duration of the imperial regime, despite its vicissitudes, and so in this sense the national polity of China can be said to be unchanging up to the establishment of the republic in the early twentieth century. Since the imperial court was the model for élite households, they, too, adhered to Taoism within the family, but conducted themselves in public along Confucian lines. The Chinese people were in that respect polytheists, in that they believed in more than one religion. Many of the more modern members of China's upper classes now follow Christianity rather than Confucianism.

In Japan the situation is hardly any different. What the Japanese have instead of Taoism is Shinto. Shinto claims to be the ancient indigenous religion of the country, as does Taoism in China. It is also the religion of the imperial family. In general in Japanese households there are not many people who believe in Shinto, but not many would repudiate it either. In Japan Taoism hardly exists, except in a few districts. In China early Taoism sought out mystics with powers relating to eternal youth, and so it came to be known as *Shentaojiao* (*shintokyo* in Japanese), meaning 'the teaching of the way of the gods'. Afterwards the word *shen*, meaning gods, was removed, and it came to be called just *taojiao* (*dokyo* in Japanese), meaning 'the teaching of the way'. In the case of the word used for Japanese Shinto it is the final part of the compound, *jiao* (*kyo*), meaning 'teaching', that has gone, leaving just 'the way of the gods'. This might lead us to think that Shinto is the Japanese version of Taoism. Research by scholars, however, suggests that there is little relationship between the two. However, in as far as the essence of Taoism is the indigenous religious belief conceived and believed in by the ordinary people of that area, then Shinto, with its emphasis on the significance of being indigenous to Japan, is endowed with the essence of Taoism, and can probably at least be said to be the Japanese counterpart of Taoism.

While Buddhism and Confucianism were introduced from China and became the spiritual backbone of Japan, it is inconceivable that

Taoism alone should have had no influence on Japan. It may well be that in its process of introduction it skilfully masqueraded as Shinto, coolly presenting itself as an indigenous religion, but it must be acknowledged that such a masquerade is indeed very 'Taoist'. Confucianism, on the other hand, just like in China, established itself as the religion of the government in Japan as well, and at least from the Tokugawa period Japan's political philosophy depended heavily on Confucianism. From the Meiji period in particular, the Imperial Rescript on Education, which can be thought of as a sacred text of Japanese Confucianism, became the Bible, as it were, of the education of the Japanese people. Even the emperor swore to adhere to it. Despite this all the ceremonies conducted by the imperial family were Shinto rites. As a result the Japanese emperor, like the Chinese emperor, in discharging his duties as the head of government during the day acted as an adherent of Confucianism, and at night, within his own household, behaved according to the dictates of Shinto (or like a believer of Taoism). This dual character of the Japanese and Chinese emperors was something the two countries had in common prior to China's becoming a republic.

In both China and Japan, therefore, trends in earthly existence have to be explained by Confucianism. Confucianism sets a value on hierarchical relationships. Within the family this means reverence for parents, and for elder brothers and sisters. Where consideration is extended to deceased family members, it means reverence for ancestors. Outside the family reverence is owed to those with a higher social ranking. The Japanese or Chinese emperors are revered, and then members of the upper classes and one's superiors at work too. Confucianism is a creed based on feelings of respect for those above one. As Weber noted, Confucianism is almost as rational a religion as Protestantism, but these feelings of respect for superiors introduced into Confucianism elements of irrationality. Superiors are not necessarily always worthy of respect. What, then, happens with a superior who is not worthy of respect? Most Confucianists do not face up to this question. They are more likely to close their eyes and keep silent on it to the end. It was this behaviour of this kind that became a source of irrationality in Asia. As I have already paraphrazed, Hegel said: 'the people do not possess any sense of pride in themselves. They think of themselves as born only to pull the carriage of imperial power in all its majesty'.

In this ethic of hierarchical relationships loyalty is the virtue that has to be manifested in behaviour towards one's social superiors. There was a huge difference in what was actually meant by loyalty between the world of Confucius, with its longstanding desire for rule by literati and philosophers, and that of Japan, which had become a society under military rule. The Chinese character used to represent loyalty consists of two parts that mean 'inside the heart'. This is because people had to be loyal within their own hearts, i.e. in their thoughts. Any difference between one's own ideas and those of one's sovereign would create an untenable situation, and the retainer would resign his post, leave the city, and pass the remainder of his life quietly without office as a member of the literati. This was the loyalty of China, or rather that of Confucius himself. There was a period in Japan as well, prior to the rise of Bushido (the principle of samurai), when loyalty was interpreted in the same way. When Japan came to be ruled by the shoguns, however, Japan's generals ceased to be satisfied with the conduct of those beneath them. Subordinates had to kill themselves in order to prove their loyalty. There was clearly no freedom of thought in Japan. Since Confucius himself was a humanist, and had himself toiled in government service, his interpretation of loyalty contained a far greater element of humanity than that of the Japanese Confucian scholars of the Tokugawa period.

This was related to the concept of heaven. In China it was believed that heaven was always right, and that in human society it was the emperor who was closest to heaven. Should the emperor err and act in contravention of the way of heaven, then heaven would rebuke the emperor, and in some cases decree a change of emperor. This was how dynasties changed. While the existence of heaven was the ultimate guarantor of the existence of reason, therefore, it at the same time sanctioned revolution. In ancient Japan, however, the ruling classes, that is to say those associated with the imperial family, perceived heaven as a source of danger, and hence denied its existence. They believed not that the emperor existed close to heaven, but that he was heaven itself. The word for emperor thus underwent a name change, from the Chinese term *huangdi* (*kotei* in Japanese), to the Japanese word *tenno*, meaning 'heavenly emperor'. Of course the title *tenno* was a term of Taoist origin, and had come from China, where it had been used to refer to the divinity of the Pole Star. However, the concept of the divinity of the Japanese emperor was already well established by the time the term was introduced, and separate terms such as *arahitogami* and *akitsumikami*, both meaning 'living god' or 'manifest god', continued to be used from the time of the founding of Japan (around the middle of the seventh century). This concept of imperial divinity lasted until the Showa Emperor himself issued a statement denying his divinity in response to the Occupation authorities at the end of the Second World War.

Apart from virtue in the conduct of superior-inferior relationships, Confucianism also emphasizes virtues with respect to horizontal relationships of equality. Virtues of importance here are benevolence, justice, propriety, knowledge and trust, and in the Imperial Rescript on Education both knowledge and sincerity were mentioned in the phrases 'there has to be mutual trust between friends' and 'engage in study, learn from work and acquire knowledge'. In as far as people adhering to the precepts of the Imperial Rescript on Education could be regarded as having good manners as members of the people, there was no need to make any special mention in the Rescript of propriety. The fact that the Rescript makes no mention, however, of either benevolence or justice shows the difference between Japan's Confucianism and that of China, as Confucius perceived benevolence as the most important of the Confucian virtues. In the case of justice there has to be an unchanging and universal yardstick wherewith to judge whether or not something is correct, such as the absolute nature of any imperial decree. In China this virtue was thought to be bestowed by heaven. In Japan, where the existence of heaven was not recognized, all good and evil was determined in accordance with the imperial will. In a Japan like this, there could be absolutely no understanding of Kantian philosophy, and any recognition of Kant's ideas would be likely to entail denial of the emperor. Thus justice and knowledge, with their inability to think deeply, were nothing but simple accumulations of information. Chinese Confucianism, which had separated the emperor from the concept of heaven, has been able to coexist with modern thought, while Japanese Confucianism, with its equation of emperor and heaven, has only been able to become a quasi-modern creed, though it may still have been the driving force behind Japan's modernization. We can probably say with some certainty now that China is far more Western than Japan.

It is important to consider the nature of the 'righteousness' that determines the ethic between people in a horizontal relationship.

Where there are two people who have equally served the interests of righteousness, what is the logic behind any attempt to choose between them? When we consider this issue, questions of competition and efficiency come to the surface. It is this that provides the basis of modern capitalism. A Confucian society is one society that has a rationality (albeit with some flaws), and the reason why such a society has not been able to give rise to a modern democratic society is that it has been unable to introduce a theory of competition of the kind that might cope with horizontal relationships. It was through its interpretation of vertical relationships that Confucianism related to economic life in the real world. Weber failed to recognize that there existed separate Chinese and Japanese interpretations of these vertical, hierarchical relationships, and concluded that while Confucianism was a rational, this-worldly doctrine, it did not have the capacity to promote capitalism. Even so, he did take the vague attitude that, given the upsurge of capitalism in Japan at that time, it was not impossible that a similar situation might occur in China in the future. My own work, by contrast, has made it clear that the difference between Japanese Confucianism, with its nationalist interpretation of the concept of loyalty, and the more humanistic Chinese interpretation (which is in terms of an interpretation of Confucius' own thought more correct) resulted in differences in the extent of interest in modern science and modern industry, as a result of the differing attitudes to weaponry. This resulted on the one hand in a growing proximity to modern capitalism, and on the other almost no movement in this direction. I have discussed the differences in the development of China and Japan in Asia in the late nineteenth and early twentieth centuries using the argument that Weber applied to Christianity, namely that even where the tenets of a religion or ethical doctrine are identical, minute differences in interpretation can bring about enormous differences in the nature of their influence in the real world.

The result of this was that the capitalism that developed in Japan was a capitalism from above with the central government at its core. By contrast the Chinese economy was a economy of horizontal people who were skilled in commerce, just like the overseas Chinese merchants. The Japanese government wanted to plunder it. It lacked any strength to guide this kind of economy. It was this scenario that produced Japan's aggression against China. The initial advances were economic, but later there was a shift to military aggression. Before the

Chinese people could successfully resist this aggression from outside, they had to surmount their own internal struggles, which had resulted in the creation of a small number of rich people and a large number of poor ones. Moreover, even the rich were forced into slavery by the struggles against the outside world and the war. After the war the Chinese considered that it was essential for them to have a top-down economy. This was one reason why communism and socialism became the ideology of postwar China. From the perspective of those watching China from the view point of capitalism, this economy was nothing but a surrogate capitalism from above, and it certainly delivered results significant enough to warrant special mention as long as the world continues to exist. If we take into account that Chinese Confucianism was rendered powerless in the fight against Japan and the other imperialist countries, and that it was the Chinese Communist Party that played the major role in postwar economic reconstruction, then the fierce criticism levelled by the communists against Confucianism and Confucius himself, at least for a time, is very understandable.

However, if we compare the economic ethic of communism with Chinese Confucianism, we will see that the hierarchical relations stressed in communism resemble more closely Japanese Confucianism than its Chinese counterpart. It is very strict regarding people's loyalty to the party leadership, so much so that in any instance where an individual's conscience will not allow him to go along with something, it is not just a question of the matter being finished by the individual's retiring, but having to obey the dictates of the party even though it may go against his conscience to do so. This kind of strict discipline may well have been essential in the early days of building up the economy, but once the basis of the economy has to some degree been laid, they have to be relaxed. For that the central Confucian virtue of 'benevolence' needs to be emphasized. In terms of human relation-ships, 'benevolence' means acting with generosity. In other words, it is almost like talking of human love. People experience this kind of human love at first hand within the context of the family. Within the family children first learn about filial piety towards their parents and obedience towards older brothers and sisters. The human love learnt through such concrete personal experience is different from the love of humanity poured into with no experience. Confucianism emphasizes that benevolence is built through the accumulation of personal experience. In that sense the family is very important. Confucianism thinks first about the individual, then thinks about the family, then the native village, then the state and finally about mankind as a whole. In that sense it is the total opposite of the process of Western thought, which starts rationally from the universal, and then moves towards the individual cases. Confucianism, however, attempts to achieve an understanding of ethics not through rationality, but through experience. The Confucian family is the polar opposite of Trotsky's version, with its depiction of family relationships totally in conflict with socialism and communism. In that sense Confucian thought is important for the Chinese so as to reinforce their socialist ideas. China's own version of socialism has had to be one that synthesizes and incorporates elements of Confucianism, rather than being critical of it.

On the other hand, moreover, the horizontal relationships of socialism are relations of cooperation, and not the competitive ones of capitalism. At first glance such cooperation would seem to be a good thing, and competition often seems hard to accept, especially where it entails a process of eliminating the defeated. However, the absence of any rival plan or opposing force is the root of stagnation. This is why Western-style socialism has accepted a competitive type of socialism. What is meant by the term 'competitive socialism' here is a system whereby society does not merely comply with directions from above, but proposals from below compete with plans from above, and whichever one is thought to be better is then adopted. If state plans are understood to be inefficient, they are modified or withdrawn. Contemporary economic theory regards this kind of competitive socialism as having almost the same results as competitive capitalism. From that perspective socialism and capitalism are not opposing systems. They can be regarded as two competitive systems – systems that aim to seek more efficient outcomes through competition – which may have different labels, but whose essential differences are not very great. The Chinese economy is now at a stage where it is opening up to competition. This is just like Japan which, having rebuilt following defeat, is currently trying to make the transition from capitalism from above to capitalism from below. Whatever the case, Confucianism is likely to become all the more 'aggressive' as a result of its incorporation into socialism. Just as Protestants worked to build up their material interests in a very positive manner because they thought of their work as a calling (i.e. a God-given work), Confucianists, too, are likely to take up positively the challenge of building society under socialism.

III

Introducing the principle of competition is relatively easy as far as an economy is concerned. Much harder is introducing this principle into politics. Some people will probably say that the principle of competition is already to some extent being introduced into politics. It is certainly true that because politicians are chosen in democratic elections the individual politicians are those who have been victorious in competition. In that sense, the principle of competition is already being introduced. What I am concerned with, however, is not competition between individuals. The problem is competition between one party and another. In this context there are certainly opposition parties in Japan, and there are probably those who would say that they exist in China as well. What concerns me, however, is whether or not they compete with each other in the area of policy. This is an extremely important issue, because in any country the ruling party at any time does not want there to be a strong opposition party, preferring a one-party dictatorship. If we bear in mind the fact that enterprises in a freely competitive economy would like to be able to monopolize the market, we must acknowledge that it is quite natural that this should be the case in politics. However, the question of whether or not there is a strong opposition capable of taking over from the current government is always very important for any country. Without that kind of opposition, the country's political world is not reliable; it can go only one direction.

I would contend that neither China nor Japan have opposition parties, because to be an opposition party, a party must satisfy the following conditions. It must first of all have a 'shadow cabinet', and the members of that shadow cabinet must operate on the same basis as the members of the actual cabinet, and be treated almost the same by the country. A real cabinet opens up its discussions and debates policy, and a shadow cabinet should open up its discussions and draft policy just as rigorously. At election time both the actual cabinet of the party in power and the shadow cabinet of the opposition should state publicly the policies that they would be likely to implement should they win the election, so that the electors could show by their votes which they preferred to support. An opposition party that lacks the ability to define policy, whose policy is lacking in any sphere, disqualifies itself even as an opposition party. If people come to keep a strict eye on the opposition parties, the party in government will also become subject to strict scrutiny. This will result in an improvement in the quality of the country's politicians. The leader of the party that wins at the time of the election contest should become prime minister, and no one else can fill that office. British party politics are broadly conducted along these actual lines.

There exists in Japan a generally accepted idea that because China is a communist country it must also be a dictatorship, whereas Japan, as a capitalist country, must also be democratic. However, the kind of political structure that I have described above does not exist in Japan either. Certainly there are cabinets chosen through elections, but the leader of the winning party does not necessarily become prime minister. Parties themselves tend to be subdivided into 'parties within parties' (factions). Should a faction other than that to which the party leader belongs acquire more diet members at the time of the election, this will change the balance of power within the party, and the prime minister is likely to be chosen from the new dominant faction. Thus while it may be the elected party it is unable prior to the election to present to the electorate any outline of policies that it might implement after an election. Elections have thus ended up as procedures totally devoid of any public commitment. In addition to this, the fact that the party in power is not united makes the opposition parties think that they do not need to be united either. There is thus a plethora of opposition parties of roughly the same size. It goes without saying that there is no question of their having any plan to unite against the government. This means that if the ruling party by chance finds itself as the result of an election unable to command a majority of those elected, each of the opposition parties will hastily discuss whether or not it is possible for it to cooperate with it for a while. Circumstances of this kind are rare, but where they do appear the result is political power without a policy programme. They therefore end up implementing policies for which they do not know whether there is public support or not.

Given these circumstances, there are politicians in Japan, but they are not what I would call 'real politicians'. What I mean by a 'real politicians' is someone who will bring about political innovations in society or the state. Schumpeter referred to those who thought up innovations in industry as entrepreneurs, and politicians are the entrepreneurs of society. In many cases industrial innovation means innovation in relation to technology, and political innovation is often innovation in relation to organization, that is to say organizational innovation. A real politician is one who takes up a new conception of this kind, draws up a programme for its realization, seeks support for it in an election, and tries to implement it in his own government. Mao Zedong was just that sort of a politician, and Margaret Thatcher, too, was of that kind. Thatcher's privatization programme was a fresh new policy as far as modern Western Europe was concerned, even though there had been a precedent in Matsukata Masayoshi's policies in early Meiji Japan. The result was to give a new vitality to British society. By contrast Japan's politicians now are totally lacking in this kind of innovative idea. Almost the only example where there has been one is Tanaka Kakuei's *Plan for Reconstruction of the Japanese Archipelago*, which ended in failure. All the other politicians do is act as messengers, listening to the demands of influential people in their own constituencies, feeding them into government policy, and bringing back part of the fruits of that policy to their own constituencies. In a society that only has politicians of this kind, and where there is no controversy between parties concerning policy programmes, there is no need to nurture opposition parties either. National administration is conducted just like the management of village communities.

The situation is almost the same as that which existed up to the end of the Second World War, that is in the period of 1920–45. There were political parties in Japan at that time as well, but there was also another powerful pressure group. This was the armed forces, in particular the army, and the army itself was also subdivided into a number of factions. Assassinations and *coups d'état* were also often used as means of securing political power. None of the parties or factions had clearly stated policies, and they obtained political power without necessarily going through elections. When one army faction obtained the upper hand, Japan would pursue an aggressive invasion into, for example, northern China, and the spoils would be divided between its members. When this faction was replaced by another, the new dominant faction would make advances into another region of China. So the spoils kept on coming. Moreover the value placed by Confucianism on vertical relationships was used to justify aggressive acts of this kind, which, it was claimed, were undertaken for the emperor. This was acquiesced in by both emperor and people. Having acquiesced in it, they cannot be said to have had nothing to do with what was going on. In that sense the responsibility for aggression rests not just with the army factions which were directly concerned. It rests also with the emperor, and the people as a whole, who would not, or could not, reject such claims. Whatever the case, when a country lacking in 'real' politicians is unable to make policy choices through an election, who knows what frenzied situation may result? The infamous history of the prewar years is a clear demonstration of this fact.

As a result of the defeat Japan lost her military power, meaning that the country could no longer carry out foreign aggression. At the same time, internal *coups d'état* also became impossible. With this the quasi-politicians concerned themselves with sharing between themselves advantageously the fruits of their own political activity. There was thus a smooth line of continuity between the prewar and postwar worlds in Japan. Moreover, there had at least existed in the prewar years people such as Ishiwara Kanji who were believed by the Japanese to be innovative, even if they were scoundrels whose new idea concerned which part of which foreign country was to be invaded. After the war people of this kind ceased to exist. The world of politics thus failed to create new values, becoming a world in which people struggled for spoils. Those who could settle the struggle in the most amicable fashion were regarded as good politicians. It was the least dynamic ones, those least capable of innovative political ideas, who became successive prime ministers. This has been particularly true for the years since 1985.

By contrast since the establishment of the People's Republic of China a succession of innovative politicians has appeared in China. Even so, no opposition party has grown up in China, nor could it have done. There has perhaps been no need for anything like an opposition party precisely because there has been a succession of innovative politicians. In any case, it is not conceivable that there should develop in China in the near future a British-style democracy with powerful opposition parties, and political power shifting between one party and another. In the case of Japan, on the other hand, the emperor can no longer intervene in politics, serving merely as the symbol of unity of the people. It may be open to question whether someone who does not preside over politics can continue to act as such a symbol over the long term, but the current situation in Japan is not likely to change in the near future. There are therefore two countries in northeast Asia, neither of which can be regarded as likely to change its national polity, at least for a while, and if we add North Korea to those two, northeast Asia must be regarded as an extremely 'undemocratic' region. Moreover these unchanging national polities comprise two systems in direct confrontation with each other, communism at one end of the spectrum, and monarchy at the other. There are likely to be many people who believe that any kind of community embracing countries of this kind is just not feasible. Furthermore, there will probably be many people who take the view that arguing against such a thing is perfectly reasonable, but I myself would take the opposite view that a community such as an NEAC would be helpful for all countries in northeast Asia.

This is because a community requires of member countries a two-tier structure of decision-making. One relates to decisions at the domestic level, the other to decisions at the community level. Where the two conflict with each other, it is the latter that, under the community law, takes precedence, and each country's government will seek to cooperate with the government of the community. This was the model adopted by the EU, the predecessor of other such communities, and so it is likely that an NEAC, too, would set store by such a model. This kind of relationship can be regarded as analogous to that between the upper and lower houses of parliament in the politics of one country, or to that between the government and the shadow government. The government of a member country consults with other members at the community's assembly, and on this occasion the other countries also act as critics of that member government. All governments have to respect resolutions passed in the wake of such criticism, and these confrontations with other member countries essentially have the same effect as confrontations with an opposition party at election time. Since proposals put forward by other member countries can be regarded like the proposals of a shadow government, this analogy is easily sustained. Within the community itself, moreover, we have the participation of countries that are polar opposites, like China and Japan, so community decision-making is unlikely to be criticized on the grounds that it amounts to collusion. For that reason after the community is established China is unlikely to be heavily criticized by the Western-style democratic countries even if it continues with one-party rule.

In the case of Japan, however, the weakness is the government's inability to put forward innovative proposals. In this respect what the Japanese government needs most is the criticism of opposition parties, but since the domestic opposition parties are not innovative either, there is no way of its becoming more creative other than trying to move forward in response to criticism from outside. I would go as far as to say that it is only through the formation of an NEAC, and its consequent training of Japanese politicians in the arena of the community's assembly, that Japan, in particular its political world, can become anything like a 'real' political world. The Japanese are famous for not being aggressive enough on the international stage, and any training that they might receive on the NEAC stage could be very useful in enhancing Japan's status in the wider world. I cannot say a great deal about South Korea and Taiwan, largely due to my own ignorance, but I would take the view that these two countries, both in terms of innovative ideas and in terms of their ability to assert themselves both have a clear superiority over Japan. The entry of North Korea into an NEAC would bring in a strong element of heterogeneity. We shall see later that my plan also includes the independence of the Ryukyu Islands from Japan. There are likely to be objections to the islands gaining independence in the absence of any NEAC, but my view is that the establishment of an independent Ryukyu Islands as capital of the NEAC would be very welcome both to the islands' inhabitants, and to the community as a whole.

IV

One other view of China is as the home of Chinese thought. All countries are somewhat self-centred, and think of other countries as being clustered around their own. In China's case it was something more than this, however. Chinese people regarded their own culture as superior to any other, and their own country as the centre of the world. The cultures of other countries were regarded with contempt. In this conception China had some responsibility. China regarded neighbouring countries as being inhabited by barbarians, and saw all these countries as being culturally backward. The savage countries to the east were known as the Eastern Barbarians, and this category included Japan. Manchuria to the north, for example, was inhabited by northern barbarians, while there were also western and southern barbarians. When the extension of imperial rule brought these countries, too, under the influence of the virtue of the Chinese emperor, these territories inhabited by other races would come to be regarded as tributary states. The Chinese emperor would grant the king of that territory a gold seal, and treat him as a local king or member of the nobility. In Japan the kingdom of Wa was a tributary state and accorded this local kind of treatment. The Yamato dynasty, however, did not enjoy this kind of relationship with China. Relations with neighbouring countries could be of the tributary kind – a kind of feudal relationship, with one side 'appointing' the other. Or they could also be equal relations, relationships based on marriage, or relations based on the simple payment of tribute. In all cases, however, China proper was seen by these countries not just as the centre of political and military power, but as the cultural centre as well. This kind of idea can be thought of as a kind of cultural imperialism tied to racial discrimination.

Since Chinese thought could be understood in this way it was unlikely to be popular, particularly among neighbouring countries. This was certainly the case in ancient times, when China was a unified country under the Zhou, Qin and Han. From the collapse of the Han dynasty until the reunification of the country by the Sui, China witnessed the rise and fall of the short-lived kingdoms, the Eastern and Western Jin, and the Northern and Southern Dynasties. After that the country was reunified under the Sui and the Tang for a period of 320 years during which Chinese culture reached its peak. After that there was again the rule of the Kitan Tartars of the Liao dynasty, with their capital at Kaifeng, and then Kaifeng fell to the Jin regime of the Nuzhen Tartar tribes. The era of the Liao and Jin lasted for 318 years before being replaced by the Mongol Yuan dynasty. Their rule continued for 132 years. Thus after the fall of the Tang, China was for 440 years ruled by peoples other than those of Han origin, much longer than the 320 years of the Sui and Tang combined. Eventually power was recaptured by the Ming, who were of Han origin. The Ming lasted for 294 years, to be replaced by the Qing, who again came from Manchuria. The Qing ruled for 250 years. Adding up these figures we can see that from the time of the Sui and Tang onwards there was a total of 614 years during which China was ruled by Han people, while rule by non-Han peoples lasted for a total of 690 years. Under these circumstances we can be sure that, whatever their attributes, the

Chinese people (the Han peoples) could not claim an overwhelming cultural superiority in relation to neighbouring 'barbarians'. The 'Chinese thought' described above just does not hold true.

China did, however, foresee some kind of foreign invasion. This was the reason why they were starting to build the Great Wall even before the first Qin emperor constructed his fortifications. These were strengthened and extended on several occasions. They proved to be little use, however, as far as defence was concerned. Enemies crossed the line of the Wall into the heartland of China, taking control of the country. Eventually even Japan too crossed the Wall, invading China from Manchuria. The Great Wall is a shining reminder not of defence against foreign enemies, but of the prescience of the Chinese regarding their subsequent history.

What, then, does Chinese thought tell us about the mentality of the Chinese people? Does it not show on the one hand their capacity for inclusiveness, and on the other their adaptability? The foreign enemies who invaded China were skilfully Sinicized. While the Yuan, who were noted for their valour, abolished the civil service examinations for a time, even they eventually revived them. There were, of course, examples that suggest the opposite. The pigtail, which entailed a man shaving most of his head, and plaiting the hair that was left at the back of the head into a long braid hanging down behind, was an established custom among the peoples of northern Asia, and so the Qing dynasty imposed it on the Han people. It was resisted by the Han, but was strictly imposed on them by the Qing as proof of subjugation. In many other respects, however, it was the Qing who compromised. Thus although China may have been ruled by people from outside, it was successful in protecting to the end the culture of the Han people.

If we term a confidence in China against this kind of actual historical background *ex post* Chinese thought, we have something very different from what might be called *ex ante* Chinese thought, which circulates without reference to history. It is a confidence that does not entail looking down on other peoples, a confidence in their own adaptability to other peoples, and their own ability to make those peoples adapt to them. Thus from earliest times the Chinese capital was a cosmopolis. If one looks at the paper currency of the People's Republic of China even now one finds that the denomination of the currency is not just printed in Chinese characters, but also using the scripts of all of China's minorities. The thought of Chinese people is far from being cultural imperialism. It has meant opening up the capital to various constituent peoples, and making it a place where all can mingle. The Han people have skilfully acquired the trick of taking influences from outside, adapting them to their own culture, and displaying the result to everyone, including other peoples, as Chinese culture.

There has been no such broad-mindedness in Japan, which could be said to think along totally opposite lines. Japan imported writing from China, but used it as a basis to devise her own letters – the *katakana* and *hiragana* syllabaries. The Japanese have gained ideas from imported goods which they then imitate, but they have never used them just as they are. From the imitation they would then devise something that was original, and emphasize how different it was from the thing imported in the first place. (Under the circumstances at the time it would have been conceivable, instead of making this effort, to make Japan into a country of the same race and language as China, trying to abandon Japanese and speak Chinese instead, which is what the upper classes actually did.) What they had after the importation was Japanese culture, and the same techniques have been applied to the absorption of modern science. Japan is thus capable of producing immensely refined products, but rarely makes anything that is really original. The dismantling of an enemy plane which had crashed during the war, so as to make straightaway something better, well expresses the spirit of Japan, the so-called Yamato spirit.

Nor has Japan been inclusive towards her minorities. The Japanese have forced these minorities to use the imitations that the Japanese themselves had made. Japan demanded that all Koreans take a Japanese name, and ordered them to use that Japanese name, rather than their Korean one. There was nothing to be gained from doing this. What made the Japanese do it was a self-satisfied yearning for domination. All they got as a result was antagonism on the part of Koreans towards the Japanese. People might say that this character is perhaps rooted in the fact that Japan is an island country. However, Britain, like Japan, is an island country, but is very different from Japan, and more a country of 'Chinese thought' in my sense. If we take this into account, then this suggests that it must be something other than identity as an island nation that continues to make the Japanese overbearing towards its minorities. Maybe it stems from something like an inferiority complex resulting from the Japanese having acquired from China and Korea all aspects of writing, religion and the industrial arts at the time of Japan's founding. Whatever the case, this kind of 'Japanese spirit' that is so alien to 'Chinese thought' would be disastrous for Japan once an NEAC had been formed.

However, it would be all the more disastrous if a NEAC was not formed. In its absence there would be a competitive relationship between China and Japan. When each of the countries – China with its 'Chinese thought' and Japan with its 'Japanese spirit' – tried to make its nation popular among the Americans, the British or the other peoples of Europe, almost all of these peoples would almost certainly opt for China, and reject Japan. This is not merely speculation, but empirically observed fact. In the middle of the Sino-Japanese War China requested the European nations and America for assistance, while Japan also asked them for arbitration of the dispute. Because the Chinese had justice on their side, America and Britain were quite naturally unable to carry out the role of mediator for the sake of Japan. The fact that they came down on the side of China was almost certainly because the Chinese people's way of thinking was much closer to their own than was that of the Japanese. Should there come a time in the next century when a choice has to be made in Asia between China and Japan, Japan is highly likely to find herself at a clear disadvantage on that occasion as well. This kind of thing must not happen, and to avoid it there will have to be some modification in the way that Japanese people think. Whatever the case, it must not be forgotten that the formation of a NEAC will of itself bring greater security and stability to each of its member countries. They all can obtain benefits by cooperating still more with each other. When global standards are required in respect of so many things, it must be remembered that Japan's ability to persuade other countries is so much weaker than China's, other things being equal.

V

During the second half of the nineteenth century Japan's bureaucrats were members of the warrior class, with an interest in science and technology. Bureaucrats in China were men of letters with a high level of cultural training, selected through the civil service examinations. This disparity brought major differences in the fate of the two countries in the nineteenth and twentieth centuries. The one became an imperialist, the other the victim of imperialism. It is this that can be thought to have determined the fate of both nations through the second half of the twentieth century. Japan that was defeated in war threw away its arms. At the same time, after the war, those who had specialized in science at university were mostly regarded as mere technicians within enterprises. Since the second half of the twentieth century has been an era of science, there have appeared many scientists who have been successful as entrepreneurs as well, but the mainstream of the business world in Japan has comprised 'literati' who have studied law or economics at university. In China, by contrast, as is clear if we look at the membership of the executive of the Chinese Communist Party, those who have graduated in scientific subjects have advanced into the world of politics. Can we say that the appearance of such a superstructure in China is a reflection of the substructure, as the materialist view of history would tell us? I would not claim to know the real reason, but what I can say is that what appears to be the case is that in China science students, aware that the future of the country would be highly dependent on science, took an interest in politics, while in Japan humanities students progressed into politics because they considered that their success in life would be very high if they followed the bureaucrat-politician course. This is a reflection of the fact that Japanese hearts no longer have a place for accommodating concern for society (Pareto's residue 2) within themselves, while such concern flourishes in China. Whatever the case, contemporary China is a country of military concerns (science), while Japan is now the country of the literati.

There are many Japanese who are concerned at what has happened. Such people take every opportunity to call for rearmament, to advocate the revival of nationalistic education. Of course the influence of such people is now small, but a shift to the right can occur in an unforeseen manner, as is apparent from looking both at Japan's own past, and at other countries. The phrase 'war is a means of achieving objectives' implies tacit approval of the tragedy this leads to for those who do not share these objectives. It is also a fact that the political leadership of Japan, filled as it is with men of letters, is incompetent. The situation is the total reverse of that which existed in the second half of the nineteenth century. It seems likely that the relative positions of China and Japan around the middle of the twenty-first century will also be the complete opposite of what they were when Japan invaded China. It is excessively naïve to say that the existence of the US–Japan Security

Treaty means that things will be all right. I am not saying that China is going to mount a military counterattack on Japan. What I am saying is that as long as Japan only has spineless politicians of this kind the strength of Japan's voice in Asia and in the world will decline markedly. At the very least Asia will come under Chinese leadership and Japan will be no more than a follower.

Perhaps this is a divine retribution for Japan's effacing of 'Heaven' in ancient times. Where we have Heaven, we have a world governed by moral justice. The people of ancient Japan, fearing that in this kind of a world loyalty to Heaven would permit revolution and the overthrow of the Imperial family, devised a philosophy according to which 'Heaven' was identified with the Emperor. It is a world where there is no Heaven as an independent entity. The result of adherence to this emperor-centred philosophy was the disappearance from Japan of reason and of any capacity to distinguish between right and wrong. Especially from the start of the Showa period, there existed in Japan nothing whatsoever of the 'Heaven' found in China. The military and special political police that acted as Japan's Gestapo tore any remnant of conscience from the hearts of the Japanese. Under the Showa emperor the Japanese became a people lacking in any autonomy, acting without reflection, and without awareness. Just like a dog that bites to serve its master, so the Japanese ran around on the battlefield to serve the emperor. Then, after the war, when the emperor uttered the curious but perfectly correct statement that he himself was a person, and not a god, the Japanese people for the first time – at least for the first time in recorded history – were given 'Heaven'.

The Japanese knew nothing of Heaven, but they soon understood that there were two interpretations of Heaven. One was the concept of an unalterable existence about which people could do nothing. The other was the concept of a philosophical world that as far as people were concerned was not given, but rather created by human beings themselves. The Japanese constructed a world in which the Trinity of Heaven, Emperor and Earth prevails. (Concretely, Heaven and Earth stand for the ancestor of the Imperial family and the people, *respectively*.) In ancient ages and in the period when Japan excluded foreigners in the Tokugawa period it might be an acceptable polity or national philosophy. The government forced the people, after Meiji, especially in Showa, to believe in the Trinity as the polity of Japan. However, in the international world where Japan had to deal with things non-Japanese, things did not always go exactly as intended, but in the world of internal politics and economics the philosophy of Trinity served perfectly. The system of enterprises with Japanese-style management and the main-bank system constructed for these types of industries, for example, were regarded as considerable masterpieces, while the Trinity polity worked; but they are all shaken in the period of globalization of the economy.

In the political world it became the norm to run each constituency according to Japanese-style election strategy, which modelled itself on the way in which decisions on Shinto rituals were made in village communities. Of course, sensible Japanese well knew that this postwar political world they had created was in a state of confusion. Everyone knew and accepted the self-deprecatory phrase 'third-rate politics, first-rate economy', but the Japanese paid little attention to the fact that it was only when the economic world had combined with the political and bureaucratic worlds that it had been able to become truly first rate. Not until fifty years after the war did people begin to understand that continuing the advance as long as the circumstance of absence of genuine politicians remained unchanged was about as suicidal as having a passage over, a dangerous area of sea without a navigator. If America were to switch its support from Japan to China – which would be an extremely clever choice on the part of the Americans – Japan would founder in the twinkling of an eye.

In the context of their greater awareness of the situation Japan now finds itself in, the Japanese need to think carefully about the issue of armaments. One often hears the phrase 'war is not in itself an objection, but a means of achieving something'. In the contemporary world with its nuclear weapons, however, the situation is quite the opposite. Nuclear war can have no result other than destruction. Moreover, a war commenced with ordinary weapons is almost bound to escalate into nuclear war. Should this happen war cannot be a means of achieving any objective other than total annihilation. Despite this many countries try and get hold of nuclear weapons. Possessing those weapons gives people a feeling of superiority, and keeps them happy. There is no guarantee that these symptoms among the peoples of nation states, which I can only call 'nuclear weapons desire syndrome', will not appear in Japan too. Fifty years ago the Japanese people swore that they would not make the same mistake twice, but since the nature of the 'mistake' was not clearly defined, what was at the time a 'mistake of violence' may be surreptitiously changed to a 'mistake of being defenceless'. If the acquisition of nuclear weapons helps Japan to become a military power to be reckoned with in the world, then it may well be that at some point after the year 2000 the Japanese people find themselves weeping for joy before the tomb of the Showa emperor. In as far as I think that China has a bright future in the absence of any connection with Japan, I am frightened that when the Japanese are left behind they will rush headlong along a right-wing path.

Some twenty years ago I gave some thought to the question of what kind of 'new weapon' might render nuclear armaments ineffectual. At the time Japan had just begun to have such people who could be called the new right wing. One of them stated that the reason why in the Second World War Germany had invaded France through Holland and Belgium, rather than attacking Switzerland and invading France from further south, was because the Swiss had better military training than the Dutch or the Belgians. I argued that Germany's objective in attacking France was not to make a triumphal entry into Paris, but to occupy the northern coastal regions of France that faced Britain, so any advance through the roundabout route of Switzerland could have been utterly foolish as far as Germany was concerned. This was the reason why the Germans advanced through Holland and Belgium. I also pointed out that as a neutral country Switzerland was manipulating a number of delicate lines of policy in an attempt to maintain an even balance of power between Britain and Germany in order to retain the country's neutrality. I point out how diplomatic tricks of this kind could be a powerful capability, referring to this capability as military preparedness by means of such software. I claimed that this was the only means of preparedness against nuclear weapons. This was the weapon that would render the nuclear arsenal obsolete.

In as far as the aim of both Japan and China is to assume the leadership of Asia, then both countries need to have the support of America to achieve this. In as far as America's objective is to assume world leadership, then America must have regard only to itself, and make a choice between China and Japan. Now we have reached the end of the twentieth century, however, the answer to this dilemma is clear. America is likely in the future to lean more and more towards the side of China, and it will be China that is increasingly projected as the country that represents Asia, not just in the political sphere, but in the economic sphere as well. As we have already seen, the Chinese people have the ability to think closer to American lines than do the Japanese. It is the 'Chinese thought' of China – the self-confidence about being able to operate in a society that comes from opening China's capital to non-Chinese and playing the role of host there – that has the capacity to attract both Europeans and Americans. Moreover with a population of 1.2 billion, China is the world's largest market. Once the growth of the Chinese economy has progressed to the stage where the per capita real income of the Chinese is even one-tenth of that in Japan, then Japan's decline will become apparent. Once that happens it will be impossible for Japan, with its absence of 'real politicians, to devise any new political axis, or to retrieve its decline in relation to China. One might say that it is already very late to do this anyway. The only trump card that remains to Japan is to make the case to China for bringing Asia to prosperity through the hands of the Asians themselves.

Such an appeal, however, is at odds with Japan's actions up until now. Once this is pointed out it is clear that this kind of proposal is likely to have no influence whatsoever. The racial equality proposal put forward by Japan before the last war was not aimed at removing discrimination between Japanese and other non-white races, but between Japanese and Caucasian. Proof of this is shown in Japan's unmitigated opposition to a racial semi-equality proposal, that would have eradicated the former kind of discrimination, but not the latter. The Japanese would have been very unlikely to oppose an alternative racial semi-equality clause that allowed discrimination between Japanese and other non-Caucasian races to continue, but not discrimination between Japanese and Caucasians. In short, the core of Japan's racial equality proposal was the elimination of discrimination between Japanese and Caucasians, and the issue of discrimination between Japanese and other non-Caucasians was not more than peripheral. Postwar claims that Japan was an economic superpower have been made in the same spirit. By regarding other Asian countries and other developing countries as medium or small economic powers, those arguing for Japan's case as an economic superpower have found pleasure in broadcasting Japan's status as a country of honorary Caucasians.

In the light of this past course of events, therefore, it is legitimate to argue that the Japanese have no right whatsoever to act as advocates for an Asian community. However, in as far as we presuppose this kind of mentality on the part of the Japanese, once the Japanese feel that America has chosen China as partner, and rejected Japan, Asia will find itself in crisis. Sectors of Japanese society will start debating the issue of rearmament and nuclear weapons, and in less than no time, not just China, North Korea and Japan, but South Korea and Taiwan as well will have acquired nuclear weapons. Northeast Asia will become a tinder-box, just as much as the Middle East. Should America be interested only in securing market profits from China, China is likely for the second time be subject to the depredation of America and the other Western countries.

Even now it is not too late, and I feel that I should present to you, my audience of Chinese university students, my argument for an Asian community. I will elaborate on this in Lecture 4 below, but believe that it is a proposal worthy of serious scrutiny. I first mentioned this idea in a publication in Japan at the end of 1995,[1] but there were only one or two reviews, and it had hardly any impact. Is the publication of a book not enough for propagating the idea? Is it necessary to start with action? I also gave a public lecture, and also lectured in the provinces. The provincial businessmen were positive, but lacked the power to influence the political centre. My feeling is that closer ties between China and America are in themselves something to be welcomed, but could also prove extremely dangerous should the interests of the Chinese hinterland be disregarded. The NEAC that I am advocating is not a market community, but a community dedicated to building up and developing (mainly of the remoter areas). What I am proposing is a community that would investigate the extent of the development potential of any resources in China's hinterland. And, where the existence of such resources was confirmed, to consider where, and into what kind of economic commodity it could be converted, then to follow through with implementation. (A similar development poten-tial is likely to exist in the northern part of North Korea. When the occasion offers these regions can be handled in the same way as the less developed parts of China.) There remains lots of scope for discussion regarding the details, for example, whether shares will be issued and profits distributed in the countries that participate in the development, with the balance accruing to the region itself, or whether the region itself becomes a shareholder, on an equal basis with the other participating countries. Whatever the case, the objective of the community will be cooperative development.

As we saw in Lecture 1, the Yellow Sea and the East China Sea used to be the centre of Asia. Then after the Mongol invasions new hinterlands were added to the territory of China. Any clear, decisive discrimination against the hinterlands implies an internal political defeat for China. However, after a while, as we saw in Lecture 2, a situation developed in which it was possible to provide the means of transport necessary to incorporate these hinterlands into Chinese territory. As far as the Chinese government is concerned, improving relations with the United States and playing a role on the world stage are likely to have a high priority in its overall political programme, but development of the hinterland, building the hinterlands into resource-rich areas of which the countries of the old Asian Mediterranean – the Yellow and East China seas – can cooperate, and in doing so they will bring huge benefits not only to China, but to themselves as well. It would also have the major political advantage of bringing stability to Asia. While this would be to the advantage of all the countries in the area, it would be even more advantageous to China herself. For the first time hegemony in Asia would pass from Japan to China. For some Japanese this would be a cause of dissatisfaction, but for a Japan whose political world has lost the ability of political innovation, such a solution must be said to be the best that Japan can hope for.

Lecture 4
Northeast Asia's Future

I

As late as around the middle of the nineteenth century, Germany was fragmented into a large number of small countries, the number being in comparably larger than the 300 domains of Tokugawa Japan, so that the question of unification was the most important issue in Germany. Unity is strength; this was emphasized by Adam Smith, 1776, before the German issue.[1] Then the two scholars who made statements on the issue – List in 1841 and Marx–Engels in 1848 – held very different views. For List it was a question of the unification of a host of small medieval countries, while Marx and Engels were concerned with international solidarity between the workers of different countries. Marx and Engels argued for the solidarity of the working class across national boundaries on the basis of sharp insights into the future of society, but their vision ultimately failed to materialize. By the time it became an issue, the host of small medieval countries had been unified into a sufficiently large nation state, and the power of those countries had become sufficiently great to overcome the influence of the workers who were attempting to work together. Thus the internationalist workers' movement of Marxism was suppressed by the power of the nation-state. In fact, in China too, which has successfully moved towards socialism and communism, the power of the nation-state controls the working class.

As means of transport and communication have developed, the scale of countries has grown bigger, and once the world embarks on a period of far-reaching states, such as the European Union or an Asian Union, it

129

will be almost impossible for these states to be destroyed, even if workers across the globe unite, and workers within the EU and AU rise up and cause major disturbances. This is because while workers may have a shared opinion on economic issues, there is virtually no chance of all workers being in agreement over something like rebellion. These giant states are likely to tend towards the left or the right as a result of the political inclinations of their assemblies leaning to the left or the right; this in turn results from elections producing representatives whose political colouring is of the left or the right. My feeling is that even at the time List's ideas were far closer to reality than those of Marx and Engels. Marx and Engels' ideas are philosophically advanced, and extremely interesting, but the actual world is not that advanced in terms of the way that it thinks.

Let us try and use this premise as a basis for discussion of the reciprocal relationship between technology and the scale of states that the world has experienced up until now. If we take the means of transport that have played a major role in determining the scale of states over the course of history, they are (1) ships, (2) railways, (3) cars and lorries, and (4) the jet aeroplane. A fifth element (5), navigation, is a form of software that supports the operation of (1) and (4). Similar developments have taken place in communications, from the laying of cables on the sea bed to the internet, and the software that has accompanied it. The British Empire was possible because of (1) and (5), while America, Canada and Russia were countries built on the basis of (2). The EEC and the EU are dependent on (3) and (4). As a result of (4) it has become possible for companies with their head offices in Britain to exercise control over their branches in Europe, and maintain close links with their clients there. It is the use of the jet that has produced the material environment in which, as I have already mentioned, Paris and Frankfurt are economically closer to London business people than Manchester.

Moreover, assuming that these enlarged states do not adopt an imperial structure, but make decisions through an assembly of all the participating countries, as happens in the EU, there can be no question of the relationships between the participating countries being those of imperial power and colonies, such as existed in the British empire. Nor, on the other hand, will we have just the relations of mutual friendship found in the British Commonwealth. The benefits of uniting are bound to be distributed between all the participant countries. It may not be easy to reach a decision as to how these benefits should be distributed, but no country is likely to drop out of the union. The reason for this is that withdrawal would deprive a country of the benefits bestowed by the union. As long as a government of the union composed of representatives from all the countries worked for agreements that would minimize the friction between member countries, the Pareto optimum of each country would be bound to exist within the union (though not outside). Thus the existence of this kind of union government would prevent attempts to make the union into a *Lebensraum* (living space) of the kind envisaged by Germany's Third Reich or Imperial Japan.

I have already mentioned that I would expect China, Japan, South and North Korea, and Taiwan to be the members of any NEAC. Until very recently all these countries together constituted the sphere in which Chinese characters were used, and it would even now be possible to revert within a relatively short space of time to a cultural sphere of which characters were the principal axis. It is important that the member countries of the community should have pretty much the same ethos. I have already emphasized the difference between the ethos of China and that of Japan, but that difference is a difference within the same Confucian context – comparable to the difference between Catholic and Protestant within the EU. The differences between Northeast Asia and Southeast Asia are far greater. Except for Vietnam, the countries of Southeast Asia lie outside the Confucian sphere, and have been markedly influenced by the culture of India.

We can certainly say that these countries, like the countries of Northeast Asia, belong to the Buddhist sphere. However, the Buddhism of Southeast Asia came directly from India, while that of Northeast Asia moved northwards across the Himalayas into China, where it became Sinicized. In the countries of Northeast Asia people read Buddhist texts written in Chinese characters. Gautama (Shakyamuni), the founder of Buddhism, lived in the fifth century BC, and after his death the adherents of Buddhism split into progressive and conservative factions. Broadly speaking, it was the progressive faction of Buddhism that was disseminated in China, and the more conservative one that was influential in South Asia. The progressive strain was known as Mahayana Buddhism. It was altruistic, calling for the salvation of mankind. The conservative strain was more élitist. People were not regarded as being equal. Priests held a particularly high status in society, and did not regard the main objective of Buddhist teaching as saving mankind in general, but as enhancing the purity of their own individual characters, that is, self-perfection. It was not for priests to offer support and guidance in the daily life of the mundane world, but, if anything, the reverse. Priests should not be troubled by mundane things, and it was for ordinary people to support the daily life of the priests. Priests, with their mastery of the Buddhist teachings, thus ruled the mundane world as well.

Within Southeast Asia Vietnam is the only exception. Vietnam had been under Chinese rule, and was strongly influenced by Confucianism. Buddhism was also of the Chinese variety and it was once within the sphere that used the Chinese script. From the sixteenth century, however, Vietnam came under the influence of the French, and from the start of the nineteenth century it was receiving assistance from France. In fact, in 1867 it eventually became a colony of France, being ruled with Cambodia and Laos as part of French Indochina. The result of this was that it was managed in conjunction with countries where Buddhism was of the southern variety, which had not been subject to Confucian influence, and which were outside the sphere of Chinese writing. For a period of a century, moreover, Chinese characters were not used in Vietnam. This means, in my view, that contemporary Vietnam lies outside the Chinese sphere. So rather than thinking of East Asia that consists of countries from the South and the Northeast Asia as a single cultural area, my view is that it would be much more sensible to set aside as one possibility a so-called South Asia sphere in the form of a broad cultural area consisting of Southeast Asia (including Indonesia and the Philippines), India, Bangladesh and Pakistan.

However, even if we exclude Vietnam on account of its rather different character, adhering strictly to the choice of countries with similar characteristics, there remain obstacles to the formation of a Northeast Asian sphere. The first is that recent past experience in China and Japan has been very different, and this has left a strong influence on their current populations. In China there was the Cultural Revolution, but this was an internal affair. By contrast, in the case of the Japan–China War there are on the one side the victims, and on the other side those who inflicted their suffering. This inevitably arouses among the victims feeling of hatred for their oppressors. We can probably say, however, that once a community has been established this problem is likely gradually to disappear as a result of cooperation within the community. The issue is whether or not China and Japan wish to create a community, regardless of this victim–oppressor relationship. This mainly involves the making of a decision by the peoples of both countries, and I am relatively optimistic in this regard. The reason for this is that it is apparent that France and Germany were in a similar situation, but despite this, or perhaps because of it, the two countries showed the greatest enthusiasm for the establishment of a community.

The second barrier is the difference in the political structures of the two countries. I have already said something about this. If the Japanese people were supporters of an 'Emperor system' of the prewar kind, and the Chinese people dyed in the wool textbook Marxists, then there would be no way that the two countries could build a single community. However, the Japanese people's view of the emperor has already altered considerably as a result of the postwar education system, and if the Japanese people understand that the formation of a community is the only way of sustaining Japan's prosperity, then they are likely to acquiesce in making the 'emperor system' into something purely nominal, a 'merely symbolic emperor system'. I also firmly believe that the Chinese are not so unpragmatic as to reject the idea of joining with Japan in such a community. 'Socialism with Chinese characteristics' is likely to be tolerant of this kind of flexibility.

If the region is divided in this way into Northeast and Southeast Asian spheres, we find that except for Thailand all the Southeast Asian countries were colonies of Western powers. The countries of Northeast Asia, though they may have become colonies of Japan, were never European colonies. To be sure, part of China was colonized, but in relation to the country as a whole that tiny part can virtually be disregarded. In that sense my NEAC is not merely a community for economic activity in the future, but is also characterized by being a community of past destinies. ASEAN, formed in 1967, may be strengthened into an economic community (SEAC), then this, too, will be a community brought together by history. Britain, France, Holland, Spain, Portugal and America were all involved in Southeast Asia, and have specialized knowledge about the inhabitants and economy of the area, so it would be possible for such a community to be run in conjunction with these countries. By contrast it must be acknowledged that as far as a Northeast Asian community is concerned, although American influence in the Northeast Asian area has been considerable since the Second World War, Western influence in the region is small by comparison with the case in Southeast Asia. While this may have meant that the countries of Northeast Asia have had an inadequate knowledge of the West, it has also meant that they have been able to make a unique contribution to the world economy through their own individual development. As we shall see, the NEAC will be a community whose purpose is construction and development of its own area, but it will have to accord with the principles of a liberal economy. Its ability to protect the intra-community economy through such things as the manipulation of tariffs will be limited to the early stage at which the community is in its infancy.

Problems resulting from disparities between member countries lie less in this issue of awareness, and more in the issue of actual economic systems. It does not need repeating that China and North Korea are communist or socialist countries, while the remaining countries are capitalist. It is apparent from this that a NEAC would be 'one community, two systems'. As I mentioned in Lecture 3, however, capitalist economies can be subdivided into those where there is capitalism from above, and those where there is capitalism from below, while socialism can be thought of as a kind of capitalism from above. If we think about it in this way, then most countries of Northeast Asia can be seen as countries of capitalism from above. While it would be necessary to make some systematic adjustments between countries, the differences in the systems are not so great as to render such adjustments impossible. The EU, too, has been confronted with this level of difference, and these differences are being overcome.

If anything, the problem is one of regulating scale. Within a NEAC there must be democratic decision-making, and if this was interpreted as meaning one person one vote, as noted in Lecture 2, everything would end up being decided according to the wishes of the Chinese. This is, of course, because of the overwhelming size of China's population. We would therefore need to divide the countries into a number of regions and give each region one vote, basing NEAC decision-making on the democracy of one region one vote. I have already mentioned how China could be divided into five regions, South and North Korea could constitute one region each, as could Taiwan, while Japan could be made up of two regions. This would mean that if Taiwan were included China would account for six regions, and the remaining countries four, which would be favourable to China. If, however, North and South Korea and east and west Japan were given a weighting of 1.5 each, then this would produce a balance between China (including Taiwan) and the other countries.

One problem is where to locate the capital of a NEAC. The capital must not be in one of the most powerful countries. Locating the capital of the EU in Belgium is in line with this principle. In the NEAC there is no existing country that could be such a candidate, so this requires the establishment of a new country. As I have already said, I am thinking of the independence of Okinawa. Earlier in history, when it was known as the country of the Ryukyus, Okinawa had close ties with China, and was a tributary state of China. After that, however, the Ryukyus came under the influence of Satsuma, in southern Japan, and at the end of the Tokugawa period the situation was one in which both China and Japan laid claim to the territory. Not until 1880 were the Ryukyus completely incorporated into Japan as Okinawa Prefecture. Under the San Francisco Peace Treaty following the Second World War Okinawa was recognized as being an integral part of Japanese territory, but many had doubts as to whether or not this was an appropriate solution, and there has been an Okinawan independence movement right through from the Meiji period. The present situation, however, is one in which Okinawa is in name Japanese territory, but the presence of American bases has created a kind of joint American–Japanese control. Moreover, there is the dilemma that if the American bases were withdrawn, Okinawans could not maintain their current living standards, so are not inclined to press too strongly for the removal of the bases. Giving Okinawa independence, reestablishing it as the country of the Ryukyus and making it the capital of an NEAC, would therefore result in the presence of large numbers of high-ranking community officials. The presence of these officials, who would be receiving at least the top bureaucratic salaries of the community countries, could be expected to lead to long term prosperity for the area.

For this to happen, however, American agreement would be necessary. There therefore needs to be within the community one country that specializes in negotiating with the United States. For community purposes Japan would be divided into two regions of east and west, and concentrating its energies on negotiating with America would be a suitable task for the government in Tokyo. The Osaka government could focus on work related to the community. A Japanese government with overall responsibility for these 'sub-states' of eastern and western Japan would continue to exist in Tokyo as at present.

One possible scenario for dividing responsibilities in China is the following. Cities currently along the coastal strip, such as Beijing, Tianjin, Shanhai and Hongkong, could be brought together to form a single 'country'. China's remaining hinterland could then be divided into four separate regions. At first sight such a scenario might appear to be giving too little weight to the urban areas, and too much to the hinterlands, but the purpose of the NEAC is, after all, to be primarily a community for construction, and not a market community. Initially the major questions will be what kind of resources exist in which part of the hinterlands, and how these resources can be used to make what sort of products and where. To find the answers to these questions Japan, North and South Korea, and Taiwan, must work together with the Chinese coastal areas, and the hinterlands must be given relatively large weight in decision-making. Building a community in this way would be a major organizational innovation, which would not just revitalize Okinawa, but would also be likely to constitute a major stimulus to the other countries, and the regions within them.

The first thing that is needed for this kind of community of construction and development is for railways to be built, and where necessary canals will also have to be constructed. The building of dams to generate hydroelectricity will also be required. Harbours will have to be built in places along the Chinese coast, and in Korea and Taiwan. All of these will be major works, but the provision of a first rate railway network, a cluster of hydroelectric generating stations and harbours should not be impossible given the labour force, technological knowhow and experience of the participating countries. The real problem is whether or not these countries can be brought to cooperate, but such a community could change Asia, just as List's plans for German unification helped Germany to transform itself from an agricultural nation into an industrial one. With the Yellow and East China seas becoming the inland sea of Northeast Asia, it would not be too presumptuous to dream that we might see it a haven for leisure, crossed by luxury cruisers.

II

How, then, could such a community be protected? For each of the member countries to retain its own forces could be a source of internal division. Each country should supply a substantial amount of troops to the community, placing it under the command of the community government. As of the present, the only potential enemies that the community might have to face would be Russia, the countries of Southeast and South Asia, and America. That any of the countries of Southeast Asia should mount an attack is almost inconceivable, and even if they did so this would be limited to a localized war fought by ordinary troops. Even though India and Pakistan may possess nuclear weapons, problems in relations with these countries can probably be solved through normal diplomatic negotiations. Should there be any attack on the part of America, people would have to be prepared for a nuclear war. At present Russia has little margin to mount an attack on any other country. The most important defence issue therefore relates to how best to deal with the United States.

Up until now America has been tied to Japan through the mutual security treaty. The purpose of this treaty was to oppose the Soviet Union, but it has continued to exist despite the Soviet Union's demise. The reason for this lies in China's and North Korea's possession of nuclear weapons. Even if an NEAC is formed, as long as any of the member countries continue to have nuclear weapons America is likely to continue to regard the NEAC as a potential enemy. In order to avoid any crisis which might follow this, Japan must abrogate the US–Japan Mutual Security Treaty and ask America to conclude a similar treaty with a NEAC. I believe, America will welcome the proposal as each member of the community reciprocally obtains enormous security. In fact, even supposing that there could be some comparability in nuclear weapons, it must be acknowledged that there are still major disparities in the technology required to use these weapons accurately and effectively. Force is a means, and not an objective in itself. Bearing in mind current disparities in technology, force can never be a means used by the NEAC to achieve its objective, namely to bring about a major improvement in standards of life within the NEAC. Under such a security with America, however, the NEAC would discard its nuclear weapons and arm itself only with ordinary weapons. This would mean that the member countries of the community could be almost totally released from the burden of defence. Troops freed up in this way could be used in the building of the NEAC. Those that remained would be used to deal with internal unrest, and provide help in case of major disasters. The government of an NEAC should give serious thought to these possibilities.

For a NEAC, moreover, America would be the most important friendly country. Even though America might not actually be an enemy, if America was not willing to cooperate with a NEAC its future would be likely to be extremely problematic. Measures should therefore be taken to replace the US–Japan Security Treaty with something that would establish the US as a country with which the community had particularly friendly relations in the economic sphere. Similar steps should be taken in relation to the EU. This is because we are entering the era of such communities. We may have witnessed countries like India carrying out nuclear tests, and being copied by Pakistan, with both countries seeking to demonstrate national prestige and being cheered by their populations for doing so, but such exercises are nothing but proof of their own inferiority. How much greater a show of superiority it would be to state that one was not going to carry out nuclear testing, because a nuclear attack could never be a means of achieving any objective whatsoever.

Such a theory of defence, that the best defence is to throw away one's weapons, would seem at first glance to be somewhat risky. However, if we think that in the case of defence it is software (financial contributions to foreign countries, diplomatic skill, etc.) rather than hardware (weapons) that is becoming more and more important, it must be clear that the idea is not totally fantastic. Hardware has already reached its limits, and its use will destroy not only an opponent, but the user as well. If we ask why people might want to use such a weapon the answer would be to realize some objective or other, but where the use of the weapon sweeps away the objective as well, people have no choice but to be satisfied with achieving their second or third best objective. In an era of nuclear weapons states or groups of states must abandon any hope of achieving to the maximum all their objectives, adopting instead a more moderate position. Whether one likes it or not, the most effective weapons in such an age are a capacity to pursue what I have referred to as defence through software, such as financial contribution for peace-keeping activities and persistent diplomatic negotiations.

I have already mentioned this before, but the same thing cropped up in debates on defence in the years before the Second World War. There was at the time a race to construct warships, and, as noted, Japan – or rather not just Japan, but the other powers as well – was in a frenzy to launch giant battleships equipped with huge guns. Since the ships were so large they were very expensive to operate, so people hesitated before sending them lightly into conflict. By contrast aeroplanes and smaller craft (torpedo boats) were highly mobile, and very effective in attack. As a result of the war this strategy of having large ships with huge guns was proved to have been mistaken, and after the war ships of this kind were all demolished or sold off to less powerful countries. This initiated an era of small fighter planes and small ships. We shall before long reach a time when it is apparent that defence through software is far more effective than nuclear weapons, and nuclear weapons will no longer be the trump card.

Not unconnected to defence is the need for the community to decide on a common language. There should be no need, however, to come to blows over whether this should be Chinese, Japanese or Korean. Settling on English as this common language would be likely to be a natural and spontaneous process. It would be necessary, however, for the countries of the community to develop the language education provided in schools so that every individual would master at least one community language other than their own. Attempts would also have to be made to regulate education in the schools and in particular the universities of the different countries in order to standardize levels of education. In Japan around 40 per cent of the requisite age group attend university, whereas in China the figure is only about 7 per cent. There is a tendency to interpret such figures as meaning that the Japanese are better educated than the Chinese, but such an interpretation is mistaken. Assuming that there is no major difference in the intellectual abilities of the Chinese and the Japanese, we would be bound to conclude that China's universities are far better than those in Japan. The correctness of this assumption, and hence of the conclusion as well, has now been brought home to me after my three days of lectures at this Nankai University. Whatever the case, regulating levels of education, and ensuring that the different national qualifications are equally respected within the community, is just as important as establishing a fair exchange rate for the currencies of different community countries (the so-called single currency). From my experience at teaching in England at LSE, which is a very international university, I believe that there is virtually no difference in the latent ability of young people in different community countries. By putting them in a fiercely competitive environment the quality and quantity of the human capital in the NEAC would be markedly increased.

Assessment of the educational institutions of the various member countries must be regulated so as to make it equally difficult to obtain diplomas from them if they are regarded as being of similar ranking. This is because if this is not done, we will have the phenomenon of 'bad money driving out good'. By this I mean that those students who have graduated from the 'easy' educational institutions will make a profit because they are treated the same as the graduates of other institutions which are regarded as having a similar ranking, but where it is more difficult to gain qualifications. If this should happen, students will converge on the institution at which they think it will be easiest to obtain the specified qualification, and within these equally ranked institutions there will be no competition to improve quality. This is the reason why there must be such strict classification.

In some countries, however, for example in Japan, there will be considerable resistance to such classification. No institution is inherently of high quality, and they all include students of a wide range of ability. Where there are no major disparities in the distribution of students by ability, all institutions are likely to be more or less similar. By comparison with the universities of the prewar years, Japan's universities have now to a greater or lesser extent become very much like this. This means that the professors' lectures are adapted to the average ability of the students, and so none of the universities has a high level of teaching. However, if there was to be some distinction made between institutions, so that they could be divided into first, second or third rank, then the top ranking institutions would attract only students of the highest quality, which would mean that the quality of the teaching would be good as well. The level of teaching in the second class institutions would be below that of the top ranked ones, but above that in the third ranked institutions. In the case of Japan hostility towards the idea of discriminating between institutions is impeding any improvement in quality.

In order to group students at Japanese universities in accordance with their own individual abilities, they should have to take a common set of examinations when they graduate. On the other hand, if universities are themselves ranked, then there will be a marked improvement in the quality of the students, especially those at the universities assigned the highest ranking, as a result of there being no need for preparation for examinations, and no obstruction to study that comes from students of less abilities being brought about. In Japan there is a tendency to judge the quality of university students by the amount of knowledge they possess, but what we should be looking for in the best universities is not quantity of knowledge, but ability to reason. Students' capacity for reasoning will only be honed to a high level of development if those of similar ability are studying together in the same place. It is this that is lacking in Japanese universities.

In Japan the income levels of families in general have risen, and it is customary for people's social status to depend on whether or not they have been to university. As a result of this huge numbers of people take university entrance examinations every year. Their tuition fees are paid by their parents, or else they earn them themselves, but since it is easy for a student to earn sufficient money to pay these fees, the number of would-be students has not decreased in proportion to the decline in the population. As far as the universities are concerned, as long as they are prepared to cope with less able students the proportion of each birth cohort going on to university will increase, and spare places in the universities will continue to be filled in proportion to the decline in quality. Within Japan's industries the universities are, in effect, the most stable and prosperous sector. The quality of Japan's universities, however, is declining across the board.

With this state of affairs, it will be extremely difficult to rearrange Japan's universities to produce a pyramidal, ranked structure where there is almost no difference in quality within a university, and on top of that a clear decline of quality of each university is observed. Moreover, such a change is essential. If reform cannot be carried out, then Japan is bound to be defeated in international competition. Parallel with this will be a decline in the quality of Japan's scholars, researchers, bureaucrats and company officials.

Despite this the NEAC will still not be equipped with the universities that it needs. Since our community will not be a market community, but a community for construction, the government of the NEAC will have to have sufficient knowledge of the sectors that they are trying to build up. Community funding will therefore have to be used to create universities in the hinterlands of China and in North Korea, where research will be carried out that will be of use in exploiting the resources there. Students and teachers at these universities should be chosen from within the community, regardless of their national origin. There exist universities of this kind in the EU, and they are beginning to be active, but in the NEAC, given that it is a community whose purpose is construction, universities established by the community will be primarily geared to science and engineering subjects. Under American influence there has been a trend towards greater liberalization of universities in Japan, and also towards having more private universities, but the establishment of community universities is likely to discourage this kind of trend in Japan. Education will not be something that is just for the individual, its prime objective will be for society. It will create people who are of use to society, so the people who have studied there will receive a share in the profits. This does not mean, however, rejecting the existence of universities whose objective is merely personal fulfilment for the individual. Even at the universities established by the community freedom of learning and of thought must be preserved and respected as in the universities of the west. Practical learning certainly does not mean an absence of freedom for research and thought.

The same kind of issue will arise in areas apart from higher education. For example, the difficulty of obtaining a driving licence must be standardized by the NEAC. If it does not, people will take their licence in the country where it is most easily obtained, and the level of driving skills within the community will decline markedly. The same must be true of the level of competence that doctors have to demonstrate in order to set up in practice, because the less competent doctors must not be permitted to drive out the able ones.

Efforts must therefore be made to establish a relative international value within the community for all the institutions of the community's member countries. One issue here is the question of deciding on the relative exchange rates of the currencies of each member country of the community, the so-called single currency problem. In Europe there are both optimistic and pessimistic views as to how this will work out, but I share the optimistic view. This view is based on past experience. The many examples from the past that support it include the relative ease with which Japan was able to unite the various domain currencies into a single national currency at the time of the unification of the country. In the case of the NEAC, however, I think that it will be necessary to have a certain preparatory period before moving to a single currency, during which there will be managed exchange rates.

The rationale for this statement is given below. Let us take two NEAC countries, China and Japan. Japanese people visiting China find foodstuffs there very cheap. This is because when they convert *yen* into *yuan* in order to purchase food they get many more *yuan*. To put it another way, the *yuan* is too cheap. Similarly, the fact that the Japanese think that the cost of housing in China is high is because when they change *yen* into *yuan* in order to purchase accommodation, they can at the current exchange rate obtain only a small amount of *yuan*, and so they have to put up with less spacious accommodation. When this happens the current *yen–yuan* exchange rate implies that the *yen* is too low, and the *yuan* too high. Any attempt to change the exchange value between the two currencies in favour of the *yuan* so that Japanese people felt that foodstuffs were neither cheap nor expensive would mean a progressive lowering of the value of the *yen*, increasing the disparity in the price of housing. Conversely, if the price of housing was equalized, there would be a greater disparity in the price of food.

Since currency is used for both food and accommodation, it is virtually impossible to achieve an equilibrium appropriate to all the purposes for which currencies are used. For that reason there are two possible alternatives. One is that the conditions of production of foodstuffs will have to change in both countries so that production in both countries is carried on under almost the same conditions. The other is that where such regulation of production is not possible, the conditions for the production of food in Japan must change along Chinese lines, or all Japanese must eat foods produced in China. In the same way, it is necessary that a similar situation arises in relation to housing, in order to establish a currency equilibrium for housing. It is bound to take a long time to establish such conditions for even one commodity, so it seems almost hopeless to expect that it can be done for a large number of important commodities. However, if the conditions of production of each good are regulated, and if there are at the same time managed exchange rates for the different community currencies, it will be possible to manage the currency exchange rates so that, while an imbalance commodity by commodity may continue to exist, the overall level of imbalance, given the weighting assigned to the imbalance in each expenditure item, i.e. in terms of expenditure on food, on clothing, on housing and on culture, will not be particularly great. Until this situation is reached there will have to be patient management of the member countries' exchange rates. If, after these years of preparatory groping, there is a situation in which fixed exchange rates will not damage the economy, it will be possible to move to a single currency at those rates. Until then a flexible exchange rate system will be used.

A similar problem may well arise between regions within a single country, particularly if the country is as large as China. Under a single currency where the *yuan* is everywhere the same within the country, the 'solution' is that it is advantageous to purchase commodity A in Beijing, commodity B in Shanghai, and commodity C in Sian. Such transactions are entrusted to traders, and those who do not trust the traders are likely to engage in such transactions themselves. When these individuals try this, however, they realize that they cannot cope with the physical labour or worry that it entails, and so they, too, come to use traders. There is thus a recognition of an equilibrium that contains within it disequilibrium. So, to sum up the above process, the NEAC should in its early stages adopt a flexible exchange rate system, and once the relative international price between the member countries for each commodity is roughly the same, the community can at that stage move to a single currency.

III

Let me summarize briefly what I have said above. In Europe the EEC has developed into the EU, and there are some people who think that it may in the course of time become a United States of Europe (USE). In the same way an NEAC, a Northeast Asian economic community, might be seen as developing into a USNEA. At the economic community stage the focus would be on what kind of industries could be built up, and how those new industries could be made to be successful in the market. At the stage when a union might be formed, however, the major concern would be likely to be the social integration of the member countries. Just as in Europe, problems of welfare would become an important issue, and in relation to this the question of population would also be significant. As an appropriate increase in population became an issue, the most reasonable distribution of that total population, the extent of population density or scarcity, would also become a major issue. Should the union be sufficiently matured by that time, there would be large scale migration within the union. The problems of China's overpopulation and Japan's underpopulation would be solved at the same time. This solution would be made easier by the growing cultural similarities between the member countries and the fact that the qualitative levels of the populations could be regarded as more or less identical across the community. With not just economic cooperation, but social cooperation as well, the feelings of affinity between the different member countries would become extremely strong. The love shown by the Chinese foster parents who brought up the orphans left behind by the Japanese at the end of the war suggests that the Japanese should be able to place absolute confidence in the Chinese. The peoples of the NEAC can be optimistic about people's ability to think not only of their own country but also of the NEAU as a whole as well. Once this kind of friendship is established, the formation by these countries of a federation will already be imminent.

How, then, will the economy of this wider area develop? Up until now the question of growth has been discussed on the implicit assumption that the unit of consideration is the nation state. Solow's growth theory, for example, assumes a constant rate of population growth, and makes it clear how a country's scale of production will expand in relation to investment and savings. However, the question of the rate at which the population is changing is not the only thing that limits the growth environment of a particular country. The most sustained period of vigorous growth that the world has witnessed up to now is the so-called 'high growth rate period' experienced by Japan during the years 1950–70. If growth theory rested on an empirical science basis, drawing on actual experience, it would first and foremost have to recognize that a nation state is highly dependent on the environment within which it is operating.

First of all at the start of the high growth rate period in 1950 there was the Korean War, and when that had finished it was succeeded by the outbreak of war in Vietnam. The Vietnam War finished in 1973, with the Oil Crisis happening just before that. The negative effects of this cancelled out the positive effects of the Vietnam War, and the high rate of growth came to a halt in 1970. We need first of all to note the significance of this international environment as a factor in growth. Without it Japan's growth during the years from 1950 to 1970 would have mostly ceased to exist. An environment of this kind is totally ignored in Solow's theory.[2] In his *Theory of Economic Development* (1934), Schumpeter stressed that the most important factor in growth was innovation, and pointed out that innovations were not just limited to technical advances, but also included creating new commodities, securing new markets, obtaining sources of supply of new raw materials or semi-manufactures, and realizing new forms of organisation. It should go without saying that war is also a source of innovation. During the high growth rate period Japan was in an environment which enabled innovation to be carried on in a sustained fashion. At the same time we can be sure that the formation of a community would be a major organizational innovation as far as the countries of Northeast Asia are concerned.

When Schumpeter discussed innovation he argued along the following lines. When there was technological innovation in the form of railways, there appeared railway companies in place of the livery stables that had operated up until then. This did not mean, however, that the capitalists who had owned the livery stables became railway capitalists. A totally different group of people created the railway companies, and the capitalists who had hitherto provided horse transport were driven out of the transport industry. Exactly the same thing happens in the case of organizational innovation. It is not the prime ministers or senior government officials of the member countries that rise to become leaders and senior officials of any community, but a totally different group of people who become members of the community assembly and community bureaucrats. The General Secretaries of the United Nations have almost all been chosen from small countries. This is because at the United Nations there are certain functions that can only be discharged by those from countries of this kind. Organizational innovation is not just a matter of quantitative expansion. Nor does technical innovation merely imply a quantitative expansion in total national output. Solow's growth theory, for example, gives no indication of the environment that might stimulate economic growth. Nor, therefore, does it say anything about any change in that environment that might result where a knowledge of nuclear physics might be utilized. (And for that reason it has nothing to say about changes in the environment that may have made innovation possible.) Solow's theory, therefore, only discusses the outcome of innovation in terms of a quantitative expansion in total production. This, it must be said, is a growth theory that disregards innovation.

Now if we look at the current situation in Asia it would appear that the material basis for carrying out institutional innovation in the building of a community has been sufficiently laid. Within Northeast Asia there are major producers of vehicles, like Japan and Korea, while China's roads are almost of the same quality as those of the European countries. There is considerable scope for extending the use of air travel. The only problem is that we do not have the politicians capable of putting forward such a 'political' proposal. If we did, they would most likely come from China, or perhaps from Korea. There would be no hope of their existing in North Korea or Japan. I shall touch again later on the absence of true politicians in Japan, but the fact that the countries of Northeast Asia have been driven into this situation must be regarded as resulting from America's proactive attitude towards Asia.

America has been very positive in its attempts to open up Asia. In this sense opening up means the freeing up of markets and capital involvement through share ownership in Asian enterprises. However, the Northeast Asian countries are not keen on having American participation of this kind. What they want is construction, and not a growth in commodity trade. This is because a growth in the exchange of products is something that will come after construction is completed, engendering a flow of commodities. Moreover, since capital involvement through shareholding means that it is very easy to withdraw just by selling the shares, there are many cases where this could cause problems in terms of the construction aspect. What the countries of the community will demand of America and other countries outside the community is that they must be willing to entrust major works of construction to the community itself. In return the community could promise that when the construction was more or less completed then the community countries would make their markets completely open to these outside countries. If necessary, the community could clearly state a time scale for the completion of this construction, and after this time, even if some parts of the construction were yet to be completed, there would have to be a total opening up of markets. Markets unrelated to construction would be opened up across the board as soon as possible.

Within a community whose purpose is construction the construction projects themselves could not be socialist construction. Where state-run enterprises engage in construction there is likely to be a shortage of capital. Unless private enterprises are permitted to participate on a profit-making basis there is absolutely no way in which this kind of major project can be carried out. Projects should be of cooperative enterprises between the community government and private enterprises. In deciding how the work should be divided and the cooperation managed, the way in which such issues were actually handled by the Japanese government and private enterprises in the high growth rate period might offer some guidance. Some of the state-run enterprises of China and North Korea would have to be privatized, a procedure already experienced in Japan in the 1880s, when Matsukata Masayoshi sold off state enterprises. This does not mean, of course, that things have to be done in just the same way, but it is easier to travel a road that has already been travelled before. However, the type of personnel needed in the top management of privatized former state enterprises has to be different from those who manage the purely private enterprises. In the case of Japan, Japan Airlines is one example of a company privatized in this way, and several presidents of Japan Airlines have been high-ranking bureaucrats from government ministries (including the Ministry of Transport). There was a succession of such presidents, and Asada Shizuo, the last ex-bureaucrat president, took the view that the next president had to be an aggressive, risk-taking individual – in fact someone capable of innovation. He threw all his efforts into nurturing such individuals within the company. Thus even where a state-run company has become a private enterprise, the privatization has little meaning if the bureaucratic ethos continues to persist. Once a solid basis has been established, state support should be cut off as quickly as possible, and on the personnel side such enterprises have to be provided with top managers who are possessed of the same spirit of independent self-help and self-reliance, found in the real private enterprises. During the transition period it may be necessary to have former government officials who can maintain close connections with the state, but should that kind of management become a tradition, shifting enterprises into the private sector would have very little significance.

IV

Let me now say something about the role of politicians in the founding of any community. In standard economics people are classified as landlords, capitalists or workers, but this classification is not based on the character of those individuals. They are merely divided on the basis of what they possess – land, capital or labour. Pareto pointed out that people could be classified according to various characteristics, and he suggest that there were six elements that were fundamental to character formation. Two of these are significant for our present discussion. One is the instinct for discovering new combinations, the other a concern for the whole, for things in their entirety. Inventors and the like come from those whose strength lies in the first of these two, and the advance of society has relied on the instincts of people of this kind. However, those whose strength lies in this element are prone to selfishness, and if everyone was of this kind we would end up with a breakdown of society. That society has been able to demonstrate a degree of coordination is thanks to the existence of people of the second type.

Schumpeter identified entrepreneurs in a capitalist society as being those with a large measure of the first of these two elements, those in a socialist society as tending to possess the second. As entrepreneurs discovered one new combination after another – successive instances of what Schumpeter called innovation – people would become affluent. When this happened it would on the one hand become difficult to find further new combinations, while on the other there would no longer be any need to do so, precisely because people were already affluent. What would become a much greater problem would be the inequality between people that had developed. Concern with society as a whole would become stronger, leading to stronger pronouncements from those with socialist inclinations, and the ultimate victory of socialist parties in elections. The capitalism that had steadily developed up to that point would be transformed into socialism. This was the logic behind the change of system from capitalism to socialism put forward by Schumpeter in his *Capitalism, Socialism, Democracy* (1942).

Contained in this argument, however, is a pair of assumptions. The first assumption is that the pursuit of new combinations is carried out by those who have no concern for society, and private entrepreneurs are defined on the basis of this assumption. The second assumption is that there do not exist people who combine the pursuit of new combinations with concern for society, or, to put it another way, who will seek out new combinations because of their concern for society. These two assumptions are implicity linked together in Schumpeter's analysis. Pareto himself, however, did not make such assumptions. He denies the second assumption and admits of the fact that there may be persons of mixed character.

It is clearly politicians who are the people for whom the second assumption is an issue. Politicians look for new ideas for the sake of society, and seek to introduce them into that society. Schumpeter's second assumption, therefore, is an assumption that 'politicians' do not exist. Schumpeter's argument for a change of system is, in effect, an argument for a change in economic system based on the assumption that politicians do not exist. Thus as far as Schumpeter's theory is concerned, therefore, the 'entrepreneurs' who have brought capitalism to prosperity will abandon capitalism at the point where it has become successful, to be superseded by those who are more scrupulous about society, those whom Schumpeter refers to as socialists. In as far as he was arguing that system change took the unidirectional form of change from capitalism to socialism, the conclusion that Schumpeter was able to draw was no different from that of Marx. It is a theory of economic system change in a society suffering from political stagnation.

That it ended up like this was the result of Schumpeter's assuming an absence of 'politicians'. In actual fact, however, there do exist people whose aim is to introduce new combinations for the sake of society. This is true of all great 'politicians', and in the context of Schumpeter's system change it is Margaret Thatcher who is this kind of person. Margaret Thatcher introduced the privatization of state-run enterprises as a means of blocking socialism. This was clearly a combination of both the residue of new combinations and the residue of concern for society identified by Pareto. Thatcher was thus a 'politician' in the sense ignored by Schumpeter. Her appearance was decisive in altering the direction of the system change. She started the economy moving in reverse, from socialism towards capitalism. The irreversible system change proposed by Marx and Schumpeter was thus halted and even reversed or at least halted. At the same time since the Thatcher era politics in England at least have no longer stagnated. Even the opposition Labour Party, which up to that time emphasized only the instinct (or 'residue' in Pareto's terminology) for the persistence of aggregates, emphasized the instinct for new combinations when it came to choosing its leader. Blair is opening up a new path different from that of Thatcherism.

It would seem natural to incorporate 'politicians' into any theory of system change. This is because if society stagnates to such an extent that a change in the economic system is necessary, there is bound to be a search for new political combinations. There are bound to appear people engaged in political activity, i.e. activity aimed at finding new combinations for the sake of society. Despite this, economists often tend to go along with the assumption that political activity does not exist. This is a tradition that dates back to Marx. For Marx the hypothesis that the substructure (the economy) influenced the super-structure (politics), and not vice versa, was a prerequisite for establishing the autonomy of economics. Such an assumption must in the end be one purely of convenience, but for communists it is a fatal assumption. This is because they are thinking that it is politics that can change the economy.

One person who was keenly aware that the superstructure can exert an influence on the substructure was Mao Zedong. Mao groped for new combinations in the superstructure and implemented the revolution in the superstructure that we call the Cultural Revolution. By doing this he was attempting to renovate the substructure. Similar implications can be found in his 'theory of contradictions'. This shows that Mao was a politician in the sense that I have defined the word above, namely someone who was searching for new combinations for the sake of society as a whole. To spell out the implications of this in relation to what I am talking about, building a Northeast Asian community is a task for politicians, and the changes in the superstructure that result from any such action will stimulate economic activity in the member countries of the NEAC, and produce change in the substructure. In communist terms, this would mean a revolution in the superstructure bringing about a revolution in the substructure. In Schumpeterian terms, it would mean excising Schumpeter's assumption of there being no politicians, for the sake of a situation in which 'politicians' can change the environment within which 'entrepreneurs' work, and providing them with new locations for their activities. It would not be a question of the economy of the nation-state passing from capitalism to socialism, and thence to communism, as the Marxists have claimed. The economy proceeds on an ever broader scale because of, and in response to, the development of society itself from feudalism, through the nation state, towards economic community and then federation.

Stalin, Hitler and Thatcher were notable politicians in the sense that they were all groping for new combinations for the sake of society as a whole. However, people of this kind are all prone to the same pitfall. This pitfall lies in that fact that the reward that these people desire from being successful is not money, but satisfying their desire for power. These people are engaged in an endless pursuit of power, just as entrepreneurs are engaged in an endless pursuit of profit. The more successful they are, the greater their self-conceit becomes. Those who end up becoming over-confident are themselves laying the seeds of their own downfall. Since politicians are always thinking of the broader community, the way in which they think of that community, that is, their view of society or their view of the world, has to be made absolutely clear. It is this that shapes what is likely to be their ideal view of the world. On the other hand, they have sufficient knowledge of the real world to understand the gap that exists between the reality and their ideal. Their constant thought is how to make things nearer to their ideal, and they grope for new combinations to try and realize this. We refer to politicians of this type as conviction politicians. All politicians worth their salt satisfy these conditions.

The more successful politicians are, the more confident they become. To prevent themselves from becoming over-confident, politicians have to be realistic. They have to keep their thoughts tied to reality, not be over-zealous in the pursuit of ideals, avoid biased judgements and respect facts. This kind of conduct was termed by Max Weber as *sachlich*, but it must indeed be a hard task for a conviction politician to regard the real world with dispassion. Politicians are required to possess the temperament that embraces this difficult combination of attributes. They have to be both idealists and realists. Both attributes have to be combined in subtle proportions, and it is virtually impossible for this mixture of attributes to be sustained in a single individual over a long period of time. As it is not possible for individuals to judge for themselves whether or not they are keeping the appropriate balance, such people need from time to time to solicit the judgement of others. Elections will confirm the confidence that others may have. It is for this sort of reason that politics must of necessity be democratic.

There is a tendency for politicians as far as possible to deliver visible results so as to secure the confidence of the electorate. This is not just true of the politicians of individual countries, but would be the same for community politicians. For that reason there would be a tendency to make buildings associated with the community as large and as imposing as possible. In this they would be no different from the buildings of the individual governments at present. In the case of the individual country governments, however, such buildings have been regarded as essentials, whereas in the case of the community such construction could be regarded as superfluous and unnecessary. The community should as far as possible minimize its administrative apparatus, emphasizing instead the development of real infrastructure, such as mines, railways and hospitals. I mentioned earlier the question of universities being established by the community, and in this case, too, care would need to be taken to fill them with teachers, researchers and students, while minimizing administrative staff. For that to happen the objective must be to eradicate as far as possible the bad habit that characterizes bureaucrats of trying to satisfy their own lust for power by having a large number of officials beneath them.

The community must have an assembly. The assembly will be the locus of decision-making, but there must be no question of bills being nodded through in the face of hardly any opposition. With respect to the role of opposition parties will become important. We might perhaps take the view, however, that in any NEAC assembly the opposition parties would be extremely weak. This would be because opposition parties are weak in communist countries such as China and North Korea, and they are also weak in Japan, which is a capitalist country. It is only in South Korea that the opposition parties wield any power. (I do not know enough about Taiwan to comment on the situation there.) There has therefore been a failure to develop opposition parties across Northeast Asia. This is grounded in the fact that in the communist countries of China and North Korea one-party rule by the communist party has been regarded as the ideal, and in Japan, with its emperor system, people were in the past taught that opposition to the government was not inexcusable.

As I said before, the community consists of eleven constituences. Except for those of Taiwan, South Korea, Ryukyu (Okinawa), all of them have very weak opposition parties; on the community level, there is the issue of capital, and the extent to which it should be entrusted to the private sector. In this context there are likely to appear two groups of political parties; probably six regions will call for the operation of some kind of planned economy and the remaining five call for the vitality of private capital. The first will of course be dominant in the socialist countries, while the others will have power in the capitalist-oriented countries. Then even where a country's internal system is socialist, the party in power will have to face opposition parties at the community level, and will have to conduct itself democratically. The regional parties will make public their plans for construction work, and it is at the community assembly that judgement will be passed as to the merits or otherwise of those plans.

It is then likely that experience in the community will in the future make a breach in systems of one-party rule. Once that stage is reached the character of parties is likely to depend on the way in which the leading politicians of a party think about society, that is to say on their conceptions and the kinds of new ideas (new combinations) that they seek to realise. For that reason any conclusion that we will see the formation of socialist-type parties and capitalist-type parties is likely to be somewhat premature. It is likely that we shall see the formation of parties that are a little more inclined to represent the interests of the region as a whole. Whatever the case, what we are likely to see in the future is the formation of a number of parties, and the holding of elections with a view to selecting representatives at the assembly. The party with the largest number of representatives will organize the government of the community. At this stage it would not necessarily be the best plan for countries to stick to just one party. Even countries with one-party rule will probably come to recognise a plurality of parties at least as far as the community is concerned, so as to become the party in power whatever party forms the community government. Moreover, it is also likely that in order to maintain close contacts between member countries and the community government the parties in power in the individual countries will send a number of liaison people or representatives to the community assembly as *ex officio* delegates.

Such a transfer of power through elections at the community level might well initially seem to the peoples of the socialist countries a somewhat anarchistic way of changing governments, but they would in due course come to modify their ideas. If an opposition party put forward an extreme proposal there would be little possibility of its being supported, and so an opposition party would be likely to limit itself to proposing improved versions of the plans put forward by the current government. Thus even if power moved to an opposition party as the result of an election, this would not lead to any kind of revolution, and community activity would not be subject to extreme fluctuations in direction. If the community is successful in developing healthy opposition parties – and the community government must for this purpose allocate a specified amount for the development of both government and opposition parties, as well as funds for research – then at the community level Northeast Asia should be able to realize an exemplary form of democratic politics.

Among the countries of Northeast Asia there exist those thought of as having what might be called one-party rule, and those, like Japan, that are still caught in the era of 'men of celebrity' politics and are unacquainted with real party politics. Political ideology in modern China, whether of Sun Wen (Sun Yatsen), Zhang Kaishek or the communist party, has, to a greater or lesser extent, come from the West, and so there is a certain logic to the ideology. In the case of Japan, however, the political issue for many years was how a people brought up in the Japanese Confucian manner could preserve Japan's unique national polity, known as the emperor system. Otherwise, the political sense of the Japanese people is totally adrift of the times. The politics of Japan's Diet, therefore, are totally inadequate for the management of a modern economy. Therefore if community politics could be conducted in an exemplary democratic manner, then Japan's internal politics, too, could learn from this and be considerably improved. China and North Korea, too, would learn that the change of power between government and opposition parties does not need to be dangerous. Nor is there likely to be hostility towards a community of this kind from any other kind of country. As construction continues, or when a designated period comes to an end, many sectors of the community will be opened up to the countries of the world. Moreover, at the stage when construction has been completed, the community will have a sufficient knowledge of construction to be able to cooperate in such things with other countries. My own view is that there is no great disparity in the temperaments of the peoples of the NEAC countries. There also exists within the community a huge amount of development work to be done. By undertaking that development together we can expect to bring about a considerable improvement in the standard of living of the peoples within the community.

V

I have already said that economic growth theory must include discussion of the economic environment. That Japan's economy has failed to recover following the collapse of the bubble economy may be due to a lack of this kind of appropriate environment. Conversely, the collapse itself can be said to have brought about this lack. It is those whom I have called 'politicians' who are responsible for creating this environment. As an example of this kind of environment-creation,

I have put forward a proposal for organizational innovation in the form of the establishment of a NEAC. If this proposal were once to be accepted by the NEAC countries, and they were to move towards the establishment of a community, then it would be apparent that these countries had located themselves in an environment of growth.

On the other hand, what has been called Japanese-type management has come in for considerable criticism since the time of the bubble economy, and I am among those critics. This is because Japanese-style management, with its three pillars of the lifetime employment system, seniority wages and Japanese-type labour unions, is not suited to the environment in which the Japanese economy has found itself since the bubble. At a time when enterprises have no prospect of expansion and growth, it is impossible for them to promise all their members lifetime employment or year by year to pay them higher wages. Japanese-type management has thus begun to break down, but the economic environment could be turned around if the proposal for a NEAC were accepted and a start made to its formation. Many leading enterprises would be faced with the prospect of growth, and this new environment would make Japanese-style management possible again. The first two aspects mentioned above, lifetime employment and seniority wages, could be implemented in leading enterprises. This would reduce the phenomenon of moving between companies, and so there would be little need for the current focus on the horizontal relationship with respect to each kind of work. Labour unions in the form not of industrial labour unions, but of Japanese-style company unions, would become a good thing. Unions of this kind are not confrontational, but have extremely close relations with the management of the company, and the labour union leadership acts as a management reserve, or supplies the future management of the company.

Since the NEAC economy would in part take the form of capitalism from above, it should be easy for Japanese-style management to gain acceptance not just in Japan, Taiwan and Korea, of course, but in the socialist countries of China and North Korea as well. Before long, however, the system would have to change to capitalism from below, and the community of construction would be transformed into a market community. The community would have to open its doors to the outside world at this stage at the very latest. Private individuals would be given the freedom to form enterprises within the community, and foreign enterprises would have the freedom to enter. When the Japanese economy reached an equivalent stage there occurred the bubble, and the faltering of Japanese-style management, so advance preparation would have to be sufficient to ensure that the NEAC was able to surmount this stage of development. Research on the best ways of recognizing the freedom of workers to move and stopping mid-career employment from being disadvantageous to workers would have to be carried out, with a view to expanding a labour market that has up to now been a market only for new employees to include those who might change companies in mid-career. When that stage of research is reached, Japanese-style mutual-aid type labour unions would have to change to take on the function of expanding the labour market.

There is then the question of how NEAC enterprises would be financed. There are two ways of securing funds, through borrowing and through the issuing of shares. The first of these can be further subdivided into long-term and short-term loans. The method adopted by Japan during the high growth-rate period was long-term borrowing. Savings accumulated in savings banks could be pooled through long term investment banks, which could in turn advance them to NEAC enterprises. For this sort of structure to continue supplying adequate funds for investments expanding year on year, a low interest rate would have to be established, and at the same time any shortfall would have to be made up by the central bank. Such a process is referred to as Wicksell's way of finance. However, as this process continues inflation becomes severe, and a situation is reached in which it is impossible for the central bank to engage in any further note issue, or to compensate for the shortage of funds. At that stage interest rates are increased.

If the interest rate rises to too high a level investment declines, leading to an excess of savings, generating a Wicksell process in reverse. In this process savings build up in the banks. In order to clear the excess savings the banks lower their interest rates, but if they should lower the rate too much the upward accumulation process starts all over again. Japan experienced a high rate of growth mainly through being able to weather the upward accumulation process. This way of doing things, however, is very different from that adopted in American and British style finance. In these economies the main function of the banks is not to supply funds to enterprises, but to stabilize the value of the currency. Leaving inflation to take its own course in order to supply funds to enterprises is regarded as mistaken conduct for a bank to engage in, and the funds needed for investment are seen as having to be gathered through the issue of shares.

When things are done in this way there has to be a stock market, but in Japan the securities business has been a world of oligopoly controlled by four (now three) major securities companies, and the situation is one in which the big companies have found it easy to control the price of shares. It was thus possible for enterprises to acquire at low cost more finance than they needed by issuing new shares. Of course, part of the funds raised in this way were used as necessary for investment, but the remainder was used for other purposes, such as the purchase of land, buildings or works of art. It was these that subsequently became bad debts, which proved fatal to enterprises and banks, particularly because banks would then advance funds accepting such lands and buildings as security. The issue of how Japan's financial institutions can be helped to recover is an ongoing problem that embraces the issue of the oligopolistic structure of the stock market. However, at a stage when the NEAC has yet to be fully opened to the world a structure of financing dependent on long-term investment banks is likely to be adopted there as well.

VI

I have given above an outline of my 'community of construction', and I want to end by saying something in response to criticisms that such a plan is totally unrealistic. I have already mentioned the issue of 'one country two systems' with respect to China and Taiwan. However, since China is divided into five units for community purposes, I do not see a problem if those who assert that Taiwan is part of China should think of China as being divided into six units. Making a great fuss about whether we are talking about one country or two would be absurd once a community had been formed. Then, there are likely to be many people who regard the issue of North Korea as a difficult one, but if the expenditure incurred by North Korea was initially reduced, and the dividend maximized, North Korea, too, would probably join. If it even then refused to participate, then things could go ahead without it. Under those circumstances I am sure that it would apply to join before too long.

The problem lies with Japan and America. Let us discuss this first from the Japanese perspective. Japan has lost much of its vitality.

According to current population projections (1997), Japan's population in 2050 is predicted to be around 26 million people fewer than the current number of 126 million, a decline of around 20 per cent. In addition the working population (those aged 15 to 64) will fall by around 32 million compared with the present figure of 87 million, to around 54.9 million. This is a fall in the working population of over one third. Since these predictions are published, those familiar with them are likely to refrain from having children on the grounds that those who are born will have a hard time. It is therefore likely that the predictions will have to be revised in the near future, and will show that the actual population in the year 2050 will be considerably less than 100 million. This alone must be seen as evidence that Japan has already lost its vitality. Moreover, as I will discuss shortly, the Japanese individual people no longer have the vitality and energy possessed by earlier generations of Japanese.

Even so, there is a certain 'advantage' in the case of Japan. If the working population shrinks by around one-third, then one-third of offices will be empty. For reasons of security as well Japan will have to bring in workers from other countries. This is likely to result in an inflow of large numbers of people from the countries of Northeast Asia, and being helped by these people Japan is surely likely to play a major role in building up Northeast Asia. It must be said, however, that this rests on the very high value of the material wealth built up by Japan in the past, and the value of the human capital built up in the past will have fallen considerably by the year 2050. It is not just the number of people that will have fallen. The quality of individual Japanese is also declining. The education of the postwar period has been very different from that of Japan in earlier years, and has been an education that has sought to create peace-loving individuals. This has led to the creation of a mass of 'average' people unwilling to assert their own ideas. This is not necessarily in itself a bad thing, but it means that there are no longer people capable of assuming leadership. The result has been that cabinets are no longer able to carry the people along with them, and while universities have been able to enhance their students' under-standing of existing scholarship, they have lost the ability to develop new research strengths. In many of Japan's universities a lecture at roughly the level at which I have been speaking here today would be impossible. The students would either leave the lecture room one by one, or start speaking to each other in loud voices about something else, or else the number present would from the second day decline sharply.

What, then, do we mean by education? There is a difference between higher education and national education, and what I am going to talk about here is national education. By this I mean providing children with the knowledge that they will need when they become adults in the future, and become part of adult society in their country. This implies a smooth connection between school and adult society. This is very clear if we look at the society of animals. In their societies there are no schools, but the mother teaches a number of offspring at the same time, and so there is a process of education not dissimilar from that of a school.

Let us think about the education a lion receives. It is the responsibility of the mother to play the part of the teacher. She teaches her children what other kinds of animals are dangerous, and on what occasions they should run away. She also teaches them how to attack their prey. Lion society has in addition characteristic conventions, and it is the responsibility of the mother to provide instruction in these conventions as well. First of all, it is the job of the female lions to secure the prey. They do this by attacking their target as a group, but the kill is divided up between all members of the group, including the male. A family consists of one male and a number of females. The male is fed by the females, but should he lose a fight with another male from outside the family group he will hand over the family to that other male, and he will go off to wander by himself. For him, this will mean death, since he has always been provided with food by the female lions and has no experience of finding it for himself.

Teaching this kind of lion morality to lion cubs must be quite difficult, but the mother lion copes with it. That she is able to do so is largely because lion morality is relatively unchanging, and the same morality continues to be predominant when the lions have grown up. When Japan was defeated at the end of the war 54 years ago the American forces changed the education system because they thought that Japan in the future had to be different from what it had been in the past. They gave, however, no detailed indication of how adult society in Japan might be changed, because they thought that it should be chosen by the Japanese themselves. The Japanese, on the other hand, were keen to preserve their good customs, and not inclined to betray their most heartfelt sentiments because of their defeat in the war. The morality of adult society in Japan did not change. The result was that the children educated under the postwar regime found themselves entering an adult society with very different characteristics. When they became aware of this they felt a great sense of alienation, and even despair.

As adult society received these new, younger elements, however, it sought to reproduce traditional society. Initially the new elements coming in were a small proportion of the whole, but over the course of time these new elements came to account for a majority. At this point the moral split of Japan became obvious. This new generation knew nothing of traditional morality. They knew nothing of American-type morality either except what they had learnt at school. Apart from the fact that the new Japanese believe in an entirely new way of life premised on 'the selfish pursuit of one's own interests', they have ended up as a people with little sense of any morality. For the Japanese morality no longer needs to be respected, and the level of education is judged purely on the basis of the amount of knowledge acquired. I may consider that when Japan was defeated there were some Americans who argued that Japan should be made much weaker, and in this way Japan has been weakened, just as they might have hoped. It should be added that the fact that Japan has no outstanding 'politicians' in the sense that I have used the word here makes the tragedy of Japan all the graver.

As I have already mentioned, while the NEAC is still in the process of construction it cannot accede without reservation to the demands for the freeing up of community markets made by America and other countries. The community will be a form of 'capitalism from above', and the opening of markets demanded by the US and other countries would be an opening up to 'capitalism from below'. If this liberalization should come too early, then the capitalism from above so carefully developed up to that point would end up collapsing. If the community adopted protectionism in order to forestall such a collapse, it would end up reverting to a very authoritative system. If it did not, the community as a whole would be likely to break down. In both cases the result would hardly help America or the other liberalized countries. Once the community has reached completion these countries will be able to reap huge advantages from free trade with it, and so there must be restrictions on activity during an agreed time period. On the other hand, America should also take into account the fact that the formation of a NEAC would mean that it no longer needed to devote a large part of its armed forces to the defence of Northeast Asia. In the past America was an ally of China. China at the time had a government that did not consist exclusively of the Nationalist Party, but was a coalition between the Nationalist Party and the Communist Party. Moreover Japan, Korea and Taiwan have all had friendly relations with America since the war. America could have no reason whatsoever to harbour suspicions of a NEAC.

Once America has been brought to recognise the NEAC in this way, it would be likely to work together with the EU and to cooperate in building up new communities in other regions. The world would before long be divided up into communities consisting of a number of countries, and these communities would in turn come to constitute the basis for the operation of the United Nations. The United Nations would have to be very strong. Given the extent to which technology has already developed, and the likelihood that it will become even more powerful in the future, technology cannot be abandoned to a state of anarchy. There will have to be bodies that will control technology, and those bodies will be established and operated on the basis of the community being the membership unit. Should that time come, nation-states would cease to have a role. They would cease to exist, or enter a state of suspended animation.

Finally let us take a look at the world of the further future. Once the period of construction has come to an end the NEAC will become a market community, and end up very little different from the European community. The elements that go to make up the community are nation-states. In Europe, however, there are countries like the UK that are in effect federations, in this case a federation of England, Scotland, Wales and Northern Ireland. As a result of historical processes in the past these four regions have become a single country, but there exist within those regions demands for that history to be revised. In Britain there is now developing a movement in favour of transferring power to these regions, and devolving them to autonomous decision-making powers. Even with this happening, and, in the worst scenario, should one region gain its independence, there can be absolutely no fear that a newly independent region would become totally separated from and hostile to the pre-independence nation-state. The existence of a community made up of such nation-states would prevent this. Whether they have cut themselves off, or have been cut off, they will belong to the EU. There are in Europe a number of groups conducting independence movements, but even if there is a substantial and wide ranging transfer of authority to these groups, or even if, in some cases, they become independent, there is no question of serious problems arising due to the existence of the EU.

The same can be said regarding the Taiwan problem. If a NEAC were established the government in mainland China would be able to claim that it had granted devolution to Taiwan, while members of the independence faction in Taiwan would be able to say that Taiwan had secured its independence from China. Without a NEAC the independence of Taiwan would be a question of major concern to China, but if a NEAC did exist it would be no more than a question of rhetoric, whether to use to term independence or to talk of it as a devolution of power. Unity among the countries of Northeast Asia would be realised. Unity would bring them peace, and they would become the stronger by helping each other.

Notes

Lecture 1   The hostile relationship in Northeast Asia

1. However according to *Later Han Annals on the People of Wa*, the people of Wa 'were often very long lived. Quite a number of them lived to more than one hundred years old' (*Gishi Wajin Den – Gokansho Waden – Sosho Wakoku Den – Zuisho Wakoku Den* (Iwanami Bunko), p. 88. If this is correct, the average life span of 98 years for the emperors would not be so remarkable, but in the *Kyutosho Wakoku Nihonden* (Later Tang Annals), as we shall see later, it is written that the people of Wa were prone to lying, so it is highly likely that this story of people being over hundred was just one example of such untruths.

2. The *Kojiki* and the *Nihon Shoki,* compiled at the start of the eighth century, are both normally regarded as works of history, but they are writings of a national philosophy laying down that Japan is a country ruled over by emperors in perpetuity. This national philosophy asserts the imperative of imperial rule for ever, not just in the future, but in the past as well. In relation to the future it calls on each one of the people to lay down his or her life to defend the emperor, and in relation to the past proclaims that Japan has been ruled by emperors back into eternity. This was the 'history' that was fabricated. Rather than historical writings, these old writings are more akin to religious texts for emperor worship, which appeared in a revised form in the *Kokutai no Hongi* (Cardinal Principles of the National Entity of Japan) of the 1930s.

3. At that time emperors and members of the nobility might have a number of wives, and hence a large number of children. It was not remarkable for one man to have more than 20 offspring. Assuming that the average number of children for every such man was ten, then each would, by the fifth generation, have some 100,000 direct descendants (great-great-great-grand-children). Since the population of Japan at that time is said to have been around 3 million, then one out of every thirty would be a fifth generation direct descendant. Since most of these descendants would probably have lived in the Yamato area, it would not have been surprising if in the capital of Yamato the houses in the direct neighbourhood of the Emperor's palace were all occupied by his fifth-generation descendants. Unless all these people were disqualified from being emperor, it should have been possible to find an emperor in Yamato, and there would have been no need to take the trouble of looking for one as far away as Fukui. This means, therefore, that all of these fifth-generation descendants, as well as Buretsu's closer relatives, must have been disqualified from the frame. Such a thing would have been inconceivable had there not been a civil war in Yamato.

However, it was not just Keitai who was sought out to become emperor. Before Buretsu both Ninken and Kenzo had become emperor after such a search, and this suggests that whatever civil war occurred was a very long one. The posthumous name Keitai means successor. In as far as that implies successor to the position of emperor, then all emperors are successor emperors, and so the name Keitai must have a special meaning over and above the obvious one of successor to the position of emperor. It seems quite valid – from the perspective of there being a civil war – to take the view that Keitai was used because the new dynasty that started with Keitai succeeded the old Yamato dynasty, and that Keitai himself was the founder of that successor dynasty.

It may well have been that one year in the country of Wa at that time was in fact equivalent to half a year. This is Furuta Takehiko's hypothesis. Furuta points out that in the ancient Chinese chronicles it is claimed that 'the people of Wa are unaware that one year is made up of the four seasons of spring, summer, autumn and winter, and think of both the start of cultivation in the spring and the start of harvest in the autumn as the turning point of the year, that is, the new year'. This is the basis of Furuta's belief that the people of Wa made calculations in which an individual became one year older twice a year. If we recalculate on this basis, the ages of the people of Wa are virtually the same as those of the Chinese recorded in the ancient Chinese chronicles.

From what time, then, was age calculated on the basis of a full year? Emperor Keitai, the first ruler of the Yamato kingdom, is reported in the *Kojiki* to have died at the age of 43, but the *Nihon Shoki* claims that he was 82 at the time of his death. This usage in the *Kojiki* suggests that for Wa the real age was doubled, and in Yamato one full year had been adopted as the standard. The ages of subsequent emperors are not given in the *Kojiki*. From the *Nihon Shoki* we find that the emperors of Ankan and Senka, who succeeded Keitai, died at the advanced ages of 70 and 73 respectively, while Emperor Tenchi died at the age of 46, almost the same as Keitai's age as reported in the *Kojiki*. It may be thought that by this time the *Nihon Shoki* as well was calculating age on the basis of a single year. It is not clear, however, exactly when the *Nihon Shoki* may have changed its means of calculating age, because it does not record the terminal ages of Emperors between Senka and Tenchi. See T. Furuta, *Ushinawareta Kyushu Ocho* (*The Lost Dynasty of Kyushu*), Asahi Shinbunsha, 1973.

4. Statement by Tani Tateki, in Yoshino Sakuzo (ed.), *Meiji Bunka Zenshu*, vol. 3, p. 465.

5. It was not just the army that wanted booty. Although the navy resisted the army's occupation of Manchuria and Northern China, the navy itself attempted to establish a monopolistic jurisdiction in the Qingdao area, the Nanjing and Shanghai areas, the Fujian, Guangdong and Guangxi area and on Hainan Island. Shimada, Deputy Chief of the Naval General Staff, therefore urged the Deputy Chief of the Army General Staff to be resolute in not giving up on the war against the Guomindang, but Ishihara Kanji, who was at the time head of the section in the General Staff responsible for

directing the war, and one of the most powerful men in the army, was opposed to extending the war with China to the whole of China's territory. Ishihara was a man of some flexibility with a breadth of vision, and he did have the power to check the war. However, there was virtually no chance of such a person having a close relationship with the Emperor, and so the Emperor was totally imbued with the jingoism of the bandits and pirates of the army and navy.

6. In 1841 Friedrich List called for measures to unite Germany, including the formation of a customs union (List, *Das nationale System der politischen Ökonomie*). The unification of Japan was one where the automonous right to set tariffs was absent. Unification of Japan without tariff rights was probably possible because Japan was an island country, but it did make the path of Japan's development all the more difficult.

7. According to Ito Takashi, Hirohashi Tadamitsu and Katajima Norio (eds), *Tojo Naikaku Sori Daijin Kimitsu Kiroku, Tojo Hideki Taisho Genkoroku* (*Secret Records of Prime Minister Tojo's Cabinet: Statements and Actions of General Tojo Hideki*) (Tokyo University Press, 1990), Tojo responded as follows to his secretaries' query as to why he had combined the post of Home Minister with that of Army Minister. 'The reason for that is that if we had stayed out of the war and given in to the American proposals, it is likely that incidents more violent than the February 26th Incident of 1936 would have occurred, and it would have been necessary on such occasions to overrule our sentiments and suppress them resolutely. For that it was necessary to combine the duties of the Home Minister, who controlled the police, and the Army Minister' (p. 478). After the start of the war Tojo resigned his position as Home Minister, satisfied that there was no possibility of internal unrest. Tojo thus seems to have regarded the war as a strategy for preventing domestic conflict.

   In the Emperor's private record (*Showa Tenno Dokuhakuroku*) the Emperor himself records that the decision for war was made to avoid internal conflict. The Emperor argued that such domestic unrest would lead to the insurgents' carrying out a far more terrible war. This, however, is a rather lame excuse, because people at the time would probably have risked their lives for the Emperor, but would certainly be unlikely to have done the same for any insurgent who had assassinated him (even if that assassin happened to be a member of the imperial family).

8. This was stated by Foreign Minister Togo Shigenori. When the Greater East Asia Ministry , which was responsible for dealing with the Co-Prosperity Sphere, was established, matters relating to those countries which came within the Co-Prosperity Sphere were transferred from the jurisdiction of the Foreign Ministry to the new ministry, meaning that these countries would not normally now be treated as independent countries. Togo (of a Korean origin) resigned in opposition to what he perceived as these countries, colonial status (Ito, *et al.* (eds), 1990, pp. 83–4).

9. The police and the law had already been reduced to a situation where it was not only the people that could not be protected, but also the emperor and prime minister as well. Japan had become a country that could no longer

be said to be subject to the rule of law. Such circumstances were all the result of the failure to punish justly the 'patriots' and the 'terrorist soldiers' early on.

The personal record of the Showa Emperor (*Showa Tenno Dokuhakuroku* (1990), Bunshun Bunko) is a valuable source that shows how the emperor himself viewed the course of events from the early Showa years through to Japan's defeat. The purpose for which this 'confession' was written is unclear, but it is clear that had the emperor had been summoned to appear at the Tokyo war trials he would probably have testified along similar lines. I myself believe that it is very important to elucidate the role of Terasaki Hidenari, who was both the recorder and guardian of this 'confession'. According to an FBI report dated 18 November, 1941, prior to the outbreak of war, Terasaki was identified as a controller of Japanese spies in the US (*Dokuhakuroku*, p. 7), but if this was the case why was it that Terasaki was not ordered by the American government to leave the country during the subsequent 20-day period before the war started? Moreover, we need some explanation as to why it was that someone like this was assigned after the war to the central office responsible for liaising over the conclusion of the war, and could also be employed as the emperor's interpreter attached to the Imperial Household Ministry. Needless to say it is normal practice for spies to be arrested, and either imprisoned, or, at the very least, expelled from the country. Moreover a former Japanese spy would probably after the war have been purged from public office by the allied headquarters.

However, had Terasaki been a double agent (and many spies are) he would have been valuable to America, and it is quite possible that the American government supported him both before and after the war.

In fact Terasaki acted as a spy after the war as well. According to page 225 of the 'Confession', at the end of January 1946, Terasaki received through Brigadier Ferrers, a cousin of Terasaki's wife, Gwen, an internal memo announcing MacArthur's decision not to pursue charges against the Showa Emperor. If espionage is defined as the acquisition of information by routes other than through the formal channels of government, such a thing was clearly espionage activity. This was espionage undertaken for Japan, and not against it, but circumventing the proper channels of one's own government, and obtaining information through personal contacts is something absolutely prohibited to bureaucrats, and if the emperor permitted such actions in his own interests, then he was mistaken in doing so. Since he could do little about some of his subjects being punished for war crimes, the emperor should have waited to be informed about his own fate through the formal channels. Whatever the case it is usual for some kind of recompense to be made in return for furnishing such special information. Where that recompense comes in the form of money, it is corruption. Where it comes in the form of special information being given in return, it is double espionage. If it was double espionage, one wonders what information Terasaki furnished to the Americans in return.

Prior to the war Terasaki made an approach to Roosevelt through an American pastor named Jones to send a telegram to the Japanese emperor

(*Dokuhakuroku*, p. 185). When Jones met the emperor after the war the emperor told him that if the telegram had arrived even one day earlier he would have stopped the attack on Pearl Harbor (Mineo Kyudai, *Teikoku Rikugun no Honshitsu* (1995) Kodansha, p. 293). Doubt therefore attaches to what the emperor did or did not do (and what he was able to do), but it cannot be denied that Terasaki's work clearly went beyond the tasks normally allocated to the first secretary of an embassy. Some of the circumstances both before and after the war could probably be clarified through looking at what was going on around Terasaki.

10. Hegel, G.W.F. *Vorlesungen über die Philosopie der Geschichte*, 1837.

Lecture 2   Vicissitudes of nation: a materialist view

1. Kaigun Gunreibu (ed.), *Meiji Sanju Hichi-hachi Nen Kaisen Shi* (*History of the War at Sea, 1904–5*), vol. 2, Shunyodo, 1909, pp. 310–16.
2. J.M. Keynes, *The Economic Consequences of the Peace* (Macmillan, 1919); *A Revision of the Treaty* (Macmillan, 1922).
3. Takata Yasuma referred to them as 'East Asian peoples' (*Toa minzoku*). See Lecture 3 below.

Lecture 3   The dawn of Asia

1. M. Morishima, *Nihon no Sentaku: Atarashii Kunizukuri ni mukete* (Options for Japan: Towards Building a New Nation) Iwanami Dojidai Library, (Iwanami Shoten, 1995).

Lecture 4   Northeast Asia's future

1. F. List's argument for the German unification is obvious if (1) and (2) below hold true as consequences of the unification. (1) All tariffs imposed on internal transactions from one constituent country to another within the German federation are abolished, and (2) the federation erects a tariff wall against foreign countries. Contemporary economists usually regard this thesis as being due to List. Adam Smith, however, had clearly presented the idea to the same effect in his major work as:

   'The uniform system of taxation which, with a few exceptions of no great consequence, takes place in all the different parts of the United Kingdom of Great Britain, leaves the interior commerce of the country, the inland and coasting trade, almost entirely free. The inland trade is almost perfectly free, and the greater part of goods may be carried from one end of the kingdom to the other without requiring any permit or let-pass, without being subject to question, visit, or examination from the revenue officers. There a few exceptions, but they are such as can give no interruption to any important branch of the inland commerce of the country. Goods carried coastwise, indeed, require certificates or coast-cockets. If you except coals, however, the rest are almost all duty-free. This freedom of interior commerce, the effect of the uniformity of the system of taxation, is perhaps one of the principal causes of the prosperity of Great Britain, every great country being necessarily the best and most extensive market for the greater part of the productions of its own industry. If the same freedom, in consequence of the same uniformity, could be extended to Ireland and the plantations, both the grandeur of the state and the prosperity of every part of the empire would probably be still greater than at present. (A. Smith, *The Wealth of Nations*, Everyman's Library, Volume Two, 1938, p. 382.)

It is clear that this statement of (1) implies List's theory of protective trade (2) that advocates enforcement of custom duties upon imports. Thus the idea of the advantage of forming a large common market is as old as the history of classical economics commencing with Smith. I owe the above pivotal reference to Smith to Mr. H. Furuya, Edinburgh.
2. See for example, R.M. Solow 'Contribution to the Theory of Economic Growth,' *Quarterly Journal of Economies,* 1959.

Index

Anglo-Japanese Alliance, 34
Annals (Chinese), 24–7, 31, 32, 165
   History of the Three Kingdoms, 25
Anti-Comintern Pact (1936), 44, 48
Armed forces; possible transformation
   into 'police reserves', 95
Armies
   Eighth Route Army, 36
   Guangdong Army, 36–7
   Japanese, 29–33, 35, 37–40, 166(n7)
Asia; 'liberation' of, 41–2
Asia-Pacific Economic Cooperation
   (APEC) organization, 88–9
Asian Union, *see* NEAC/NEAU
Asiatic despotism (Marx), 101
Asiatic mode of production (Marx),
   101–2

Bakufu (military government), 32, 65,
   74–5, 98
Banks, 157–8
Barbarians, 8, 27, 31, 32, 117–19
Beijing, 1–8, 10, 14, 17, 144
Bosnia, 82, 95–6
Britain, 18, 19, 33, 38, 39, 41, 42, 60,
   133, 150, 157, 168–9
   Blairism, 150
   electoral politics, 19
   Labour Party, 150
   monarchy, 43, 79
   party politics, 112–13, 115
   Thatcherism, 78, 93, 99, 114,
      150–1
   transition to 'capitalism from
      below', 97, 100
British Empire/Commonwealth,
   73–9, 130, 169
Buddhism, 105, 131–2
Buretsu, 23, 164–5(n3)
Bushido, 107

Canada, 97, 130
Capital, 84, 87, 88
Capitalism, 35, 72, 111, 149–50
   modern, 109
   monopoly capitalism, 34
   'pre-capitalist stage', 35
Capitalism from above, 56, 134
   Chinese, 110
   general, 97–8
   Japan, 97–8, 109
   NEAC, 156, 161
   resemblance of 'Chinese style of
      socialism' to, 16
Capitalism from below, 97, 134
   Chinese tardiness in making
      transition to, 100
   attempted transition (Japan) to,
      111
   long-term goal of NEAC, 156, 161
Chiang Kai-shek (Zhang Kaishek)
   (1887–1975), vii, 155
China (pre-1949), 31, 39, 101–4, 127,
   132–3, 162
   bureaucracy, 58, 121
   education, 58–9
   foreign rulers of, 8, 118–19
   Great Wall, 7–8, 119
   imperial court, 104–5
   imperial rescripts, 51
   Japanese attacks on, 11
   'mandate of heaven', 54–5, 57, 59
   monarchy, 7–10, 59, 103–7, 118
   people and emperor in, 37, 106
   religion, 104–5
   tributary relations, 117–19
China, People's Republic of, 100–1,
   129, 131–5, 146, 155–63
   absence of an Opposition, 115
   closer ties with the USA, 125–8, 162
   Cultural Revolution, 13, 132, 151

economy 'opening up to
    competition', 111
'far more Western than Japan', 108
'innovative politicians' in, 115
leaders 'not left-wing extremists', 15
more influential internationally
    than Japan, 121, 123
'one country, two systems', 158
proposed division under NEAC,
    134–6
visited by the author (September
    1997), 1–20
Chinese civilization, 21, 26–7
Chinese people, 9, 12, 15, 37–8
'Chinese thought', 8, 117–21, 126
Christianity, 28–9, 58, 105, 106, 111,
    131
Communism, 20–1, 41–2, 98, 116,
    134, 154
  China, 9, 11–15
  Japan, 42
Communist parties
  Chinese, 3, 12–15, 36, 104, 110,
    122, 155, 162
  Japanese, 19–20
Confucianism, 104–5, 111–2, 131, 155
  'benevolence', 57, 108, 110
  Chinese humanism/
    humanitarianism, 10, 107–9
  Chinese and Japanese versions, 10,
    57–9, 106–9
  communist criticism of, 110
  and economic life in the real world,
    109
  education and class categorization
    (China), 13
  filial piety, 52, 57, 110
  hierarchy, 106–7
  'rational', 106, 109
  'righteousness', 108–9
  value placed on vertical
    relationships, 114–15
  Vietnam, 132
Corruption, 167
Criminals, 32, 47
Culture, 89–90, 117–19, 121, 131–2,
    143

Currencies, 93, 119, 139, 142–4, 157

Daimyo (lords), 28–9
Democracy, 34, 41, 56, 97, 100–1,
    112–13, 134, 152
Domains (*han*), 63–5, 75, 142

East Asian people (*Toa minzoku*), 92
East China Sea, 128, 136
Economic environment, 155–6
  see also Technology
Education, 13, 22, 51–9, 62, 71,
    106–8, 159, 160–1
  in proposed NEAC, 90–1, 139–42,
    153
Elections, 19, 130, 152, 154
Elitism, 18–19
Employee-shareholding (proposed),
    84, 87–8
Engels, F. (1820–95), 20, 129, 130
Environmentalism, 69, 81
Espionage, 167
Ethics, 53, 64–6, 108–11
Ethos, vii, 80, 131, 148
European Coal and Steel Community,
    67
European Community, 68
European Economic Community
    (EEC), 67, 76, 89, 91, 130, 144;
  proposed NEAC contrasted to, 83,
    87
European Union (EU), 68, 76–9, 116,
    129–31, 134, 144, 162–3
  'forming a European people', 77–8
  multiple identities within, 77–8
  NEAC comparisons, 134–5
  single currency, 93
  universities, 141
Examinations (civil service), 29, 56–8,
    101–4, 119–21

Families, 66, 69, 72–3, 110–11
Federations of states, 69, 95, 129–30
Feudalism, 74–5
Flood control and irrigation, 101
Food scarcity, 49
Foodstuffs, 142–3

France, 33, 38, 97, 133
French Indo-China, 38, 44, 132
Furuta Takehiko, 26, 165

G7/G8 countries, 14, 70, 97
Gemeinsamer Markt (Common
    Market), 71
Gemeinschaft ('informal' association,
    'community'), 61–2, 67– 72, 80–1,
    92
  'Japanese-type company' an
    example of, 72
Germany, 48, 68, 129, 131–6,
    168(n1 to L4)
Gesellschaft ('formal, man-made
    association'; 'community of
    interest'), 35, 61–2, 66–9, 71–5,
    79–80, 92
Growth (economic), 27, 87, 93–4,
    145–6, 156–7
Guo Ruo-mo, vii
Guomindang, 162, 165(n5)

Hayashi Kentaro, 51–2
'Heaven', 9, 52, 54–7, 59–60, 107–8,
    123–4
Hegel, G.W.F. (1770–1831), 37, 59,
    60, 101, 103–6
Hideyoshi, *see* Toyotomi Hideyoshi
Historical materialism (Marx), 101–2,
    104, 122
Hitler, Adolf (1889–1945), 38, 67, 151
Holland, 39, 133
Horizontal relationships, 108–9, 111
Hydro-electricity, 136

Imperial family (Japan), 10, 11, 22–3,
    56, 74, 107–8, 123
  see also Monarchy
Imperial Rescript on Education
    (*Kyoiku Chokugo*) (1890), 51–3,
    106, 108
Imperial Rescript to Soldiers and
    Sailors (*Gunjin Chokuyu*), 51, 53
Imperialism, 34–5, 67, 69, 133
  Japanese, 3, 11–12, 28–9, 32, 41, 57,
    121–2
  'premodern', 35

Incidents, 47
  February 26th Incident (1936), 44,
    166(n7)
  Manchurian Incident (1931), 11,
    31, 32, 36, 40, 45, 63–4
  March Incident (1931), 45
  Marco Polo Bridge Incident (July
    1937), 36–7, 40
  see also War
India, 73, 101, 131, 132
Indonesia, 132
Innovation, 114–15, 117, 145–6, 149,
    156
Intelligentsia
  Chinese, 8, 13
  Japanese, 36
  left-wing, 47–8
Ishihara Kanji, 115, 165–6(n5)

Japan, 1, 8, 16, 103, 131–4, 162
  absence of 'true politicians',
    113–14, 123, 147, 155, 161
  Amaterasu (goddess), 54
  American Occupation, 42, 161
  'bubble economy', 155–6, 157
  bureaucracy, 58, 121
  Chinese cultural tutelage, 81–2, 120
  clans, 74–5
  constitution (post-war), 62, 70
  coups d'état, 45, 114, 115
  demography, 159, 164(n3)
  early links with Korea, 10–11, 12,
    26–8
  emperor-system, 78–9, 133, 153,
    155
  fear of revolution, 55–7, 123
  Heaven–Emperor–Earth trinity,
    123–4
  high growth-rate period (1950–70),
    146, 157
  history (mythical), 22–3, 164(n1–2)
  'incompetent' political leadership,
    19, 31, 113–15, 117, 122–3,
    124–8
  'Leader of Asia', 30–1, 34, 89
  'like a medieval absolutist state',
    65–6

'men of celebrity' politics, 19, 155
military and political police, 123
national polity, 51, 55–6, 58–60,
    116, 155
'Nazi state without a Hitler', 48–9
origins, 9–11, 22–4, 164(n1–2)
rearmament issue, 124–5, 127
Japan Airlines, 148
Japanese
    'arrogance', 12, 27–8, 31, 35, 57
    'feelings of discrimination' (towards
        Asia), 82
    'jingoism', 30, 32, 34, 40, 47,
        166(n5)

Kamikaze (divine wind), 28
Kant, Immanuel (1724–1804), 80–1,
    108
Keitai dynasty, 23, 25, 26, 27, 55, 165
Kellogg–Briand Pact (1928), 70
Keynes, Lord (1883–1946), 67, 68
Kita Ikki (d. 1936), 31, 38
Knife-edge property, 58
Kojiki (712 AD), 11, 22–4, 164–5(n2–3)
Komoto Daisaku, 36
Konoe, Prince Fumimaro, 44–6
Korea, 11, 16, 35, 38, 81, 136
    early history, 9–10, 26–8
    North, 15, 116–17, 127, 131–5,
        153–8
    South, 127, 131, 134–5, 146–7,
        153–6, 162
Koreans, 37–8, 82, 120
Kyushu dynasty, 9, 25

Labour unions, 156, 157
Lebensraum (life space), 68, 131
Lee Byung Chu; *Kankoku Kodai Shi*
    (Ancient History of Korea, 1979),
    26
Lenin, V.I. (1870–1924), 20, 34, 35,
    151
Li, Professor C.M., 2
Lion society, 160
List, Friedrich (1789–1846), 68, 129,
    136, 166(n6), 168
Literati, rule by, 103–4, 107

London School of Economics (LSE),
    vii, 18, 62, 139
Lu Xin, vii

MacArthur, General Douglas
    (1880–1964), 50, 167
Management (Japanese-type), 156–7
Manchukuo, 47
Manchuria, vii, 31–8, 42–7, 117–19,
    165(n5)
Man'yoshu, 11
Mao Zedong, 3, 13, 114, 151
Maoism, 15
Marx, Karl (1818–83), 20, 34–5, 101,
    129–30, 150–1
Marxism, 56, 129, 133
Materialist relationship (technology-
    politics), 81
Matsukata Masayoshi, 114, 148
Meiji Restoration / Meiji era, 16, 29,
    31–5, 40, 60, 68, 75–8, 82, 93, 99,
    104–6, 114, 122, 135
Mimana, 26
Min, Queen (assassinated), 36
Minamoto clan, 74
Miura Goro, 36
Monarchy (Japanese), 35–7, 55, 75–9,
    102–6, 115–16, 125, 164–5(n1–3),
    166(n5, n7)
    'coeval with heaven and earth', 9,
        52, 55
    'Emperor-system', 37–9, 41–3, 48,
        52–3, 59–60
    identified with Heaven, 123
    ranking at court, 56, 58–9
    responsibility for World War II,
        39–41, 43, 45–50, 115, 166–8(n9)
    Showa emperor (Hirohito), 41–3,
        45–50, 108, 123–5, 166–8
        (n7, n9)
    'tenno', 60, 107–8
Mongols, 11, 28, 82, 128
Morishima, Michio
    Marx's Economics (1973), 17
    Options for Japan (1995), 15, 127,
        168(n1 to L3)
    Why Has Japan 'Succeeded'? (1982), 58

Nakrang (Korea), 10
Nankai University (Tianjin), vii, 1–2,
     13, 14–15, 18, 139
Nation-states, 21, 69, 78, 80, 129,
     151
Nationalism
  balance with universalism, 63–4
  Chinese, 8
  Eurosceptics, 78
  Japanese, 10, 48, 57, 63–4, 67, 68
  Kant's theory of peace, 81
  'not the supreme ethic', 64–5
Nazism/fascism, 98
Nihon, 9–11, 24–6, 55, 102
Nihon Shoki (720 AD), 11, 22, 24,
     164–5(n2–3)
Nishida Kitaro, 65–6
Nissan, 35
Northeast Asia, 127ff
Northeast Asian Economic
     Community (NEAC), 21, 82, 121,
     134, 145
  'capitalism from above', 134
  central bank, 157
  'community for construction', 141,
     147–8, 155–8, 162
  currency, 139, 142–4
  decision-making, 116–17, 134–6
  EU comparisons, 79, 116, 129–31,
     134–5, 144, 162–3
  independent Ryukyu Islands
     proposed capital of, 117
  Japan and USA main problems *re*,
     158–62
  'one community, two systems', 134
  'one region, one vote', 134–5
  party formation, 153–4
  Taiwan problem, 163
  transformation into market
     community, 156–7
Northeast Asian Union (NEAU), 70,
     79, 81, 89–96, 129–30, 145
Nuclear weaponry, 49, 124–5, 137–9

Oil crisis, 145
Okinawa, *see* Ryukyu Islands
One-party rule, 116, 153–5

Opposition parties, 112–14, 115,
     153–4
Overseas Chinese, 109

Pacifism, 34
Paekche, 9, 25, 55
Pareto, V.F.D. (1848–1923), 122, 131,
     148–50
Pigtail, 119
Planned economies
  Japan, 45, 56
  NEAC ('free enterprise hybrid'),
     87–9
Privatization, 16, 98–9, 114, 148, 150
Prostitution, 37–8, 82
Pusan, 11, 86

Qin dynasty (China, late third century
     BC), 7, 8, 118, 119
Qing dynasty (China, 1644–1911), 7,
     51, 103, 118–19

Racism, 30, 34, 36, 47, 117–19, 126
Religion, 89
  enormous effect of minute
     differences in interpretation,
     109
Russia, 130, 137
Russian Revolution, 33
Ryukyu Islands, 117, 135, 136, 153

Saigo Takamori, 78
San Francisco Peace Treaty, 135
Schumpeter, J.A. (1883–1950), 114
  analysis of imperialism, 34
  Capitalism, Socialism, Democracy
     (1942), 149–51
  Theory of Economic Development
     (1934), 145–6
Shandong, 10, 34
Shanghai, 4, 14, 17, 144
Shareholding, 127, 147, 158
Shinto, 89, 105–6, 124
Shoguns, 65, 75, 107
Shotoku, Prince, 58
Sian, 7–8, 17, 144
Singapore, vii, 37, 86

Slogans
    'all the eight corners of the world under one roof' (*hakko ichiu*), 36, 39, 40, 57
    'die for the Emperor', 40
    'Greater East Asia Co-Prosperity Sphere', vii, 15, 39, 42, 68, 82, 89, 166(n8)
    'liberating East Asia from the domination of the Caucasians', 39, 40
    'one community, two systems', 15, 16
    'socialism with Chinese characteristics', 15–16, 99, 133
Smith, Adam (1723–90), 129, 168–9
Solow, R.M., 145, 146
Southeast Asia, 15, 38, 131, 132, 133–4, 137
Soviet Union, 50, 137
Sui dynasty (589–618 AD), 9, 55, 101–2
Sun Yat-sen (1866–1925), vii, 155
Sweezy, Paul M., 34

Taiwan, 12, 38, 86, 117, 127, 131–5, 136, 153–8, 162–3
Takata Yasuma, 92, 168(n3)
Tanaka Kakuei (1918–93), 114
Tani Tateki, 31–2, 38
Taoism, 104–6, 107
Tariffs, 33–4, 91, 134, 166(n6), 168 (n1 to L4)
Technology, 27, 60, 67–8, 69, 70, 87, 99, 114, 121, 136, 137, 162;
    'determines the size of a state', 74–7, 81, 130
    effect on world government, 70, 81
Terasaki Hidenari, 50, 167–8
Togo Shigenori, 166(n8)
Tojo Hideki (1885–1948), vii, 44–8, 67, 166(n7)
Tokugawa period (Japan), 31–2, 40, 47, 65–8, 74–5, 102, 129, 135
    Confucianism, 106
    isolationist policy, 29
    unequal treaties, 33–5, 40, 47
Toyotomi Hideyoshi (1536–98), 11, 28–9, 82
Transport and communications, 12, 74, 128–9
Triple Alliance (Japan–Germany–Italy), 48
Trotsky, Leon (1879–1940), 111

Unification
  China, 9
  Germany (1871), 68, 97–8, 129, 136, 166(n6), 168–9
  Italy (1861), 68, 97–8
  Japan, 68, 74–5, 97–8, 166(n6)
United Kingdom
  devolution, 162–3
  'in effect a federation', 162
United Nations, 22, 70, 80, 95, 146, 162
United States of America (USA), 18, 33–9, 41–2, 60, 67, 97, 100, 130–7, 147, 157
  and APEC, 88–9
  Okinawa issue, 135
  proposed NEAC and, 135
  Security Pact with NEAC, 137
United States of Northeast Asia (USNEA), 96, 144
US–Japan Security Pact (1951–), 122, 137

Versailles Peace Conference, 34
Vietnam, 38, 131, 132

Wa, 9–11, 24–8, 55, 102, 118, 164(n1), 165
War
  Japan–China (1931–45), 11, 16, 29, 31–9, 42–4, 60, 121–3, 132, 165–6(n5)
  Japanese aggression against China, 109–10, 114–15
  Japanese annexation of Korea (1910–45), 11, 31–6
  Japanese attacks on Korea (1592, 1597), 11, 28–9, 82
  Korean War (1950–3), 50, 145

War, *cont.*
  Marco Polo Bridge Incident (July
    1937), 36–7, 40
  Mongol (Yuan) attacks on Japan,
    11, 28, 82
  Mongol invasions of China, 128
  Nanjing Massacre (1937), 37
  national egoism and, 63, 66
  in Northeast Asia, 21–60
  Paekson River (battle, 622 AD), 9,
    24–6, 28
  Pearl Harbor (1941), 41, 43, 44, 95,
    168(n9)
  Russo–Japanese (1904–5), 33, 64, 68
  Siberian expedition (1918–25),
    33–5, 40, 47
  Sino-Japanese (1894–5), 11, 29,
    31–3, 82, 104
  Vietnam War, 145
  war leaders (1931–45), 43–6
  World War I, 32–4, 46, 73–4

World War II, vii, 1, 3, 8, 30, 32,
  36–50, 60, 63–6, 73–4, 95–8,
  120–2, 125, 138–9
Washington Conference (1921–2), 34
Watsuji Tetsuro, 65–6
Weber, M. (1864–1920), 58, 101, 104,
  106, 109
Wicksell's way of finance, 157
Wittfogel, Karl A., 101
World (*die Welt*), 'becoming a
  community', 68–70
World government, 70

Yamato dynasty, 9, 11, 23–6, 27, 55,
  118, 164–5(n3)
Yellow Sea, 10, 128, 136
Yuan dynasty, 7, 11, 118–19

Zaibatsu, 35, 99–100
Zhang Zuolin (Manchurian warlord), 36
Zhou Enlai (1898–1976), vii, 1–2